Social Media for School Leaders

A Comprehensive Guide to Getting the Most Out of Facebook, Twitter, and Other Essential Web Tools

Brian J. Dixon

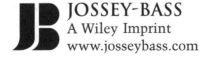

JOSSEY-BASS
A Wiley Imprint
www.josseybass.com

Published by Jossey-Bass
A Wiley Imprint
One Montgomery Street, Suite 1200, San Francisco, CA 94104-4594—www.josseybass.com

Jossey-Bass books and products are available through most bookstores. To contact Jossey-Bass directly call our Customer Care Department within the U.S. at 800-956-7739, outside the U.S. at 317-572-3986, or fax 317-572-4002.

Wiley publishes in a variety of print and electronic formats and by print-on-demand. Some material included with standard print versions of this book may not be included in e-books or in print-on-demand. If this book refers to media such as a CD or DVD that is not included in the version you purchased, you may download this material at http://booksupport.wiley.com. For more information about Wiley products, visit www.wiley.com.

Library of Congress Cataloging-in-Publication Data
Dixon, Brian
    Social media for school leaders : a comprehensive guide to getting the most out of Facebook, Twitter, and other essential web tools / Brian J. Dixon.
        p. cm.
    Includes index.
        ISBN 978-1-118-34234-3 (pbk.); ISBN 978-1-118-38885-3 (pdf); ISBN 978-1-118-38889-1 (epub); ISBN 978-1-118-38887-7 (mobipocket)
    1. Educational technology–United States.   2. Education–Effect of technological innovations on–United States.   3. Social media.   4. School administrators–United States.   5. Educational leadership–United States.   I. Title.
    LB1028.3.D585 2012
    371.33–dc23

                              2012020345

Printed in the United States of America
FIRST EDITION
PB Printing   10 9 8 7 6 5 4 3 2 1

To Julie and Ryland

Contents

Preface

This book is written specifically for you:

- **Technophobic educator.** You have been waiting to read this book. With the explosion of Facebook in recent years and Twitter nipping at its heels, you promised yourself, "One day I'll learn how to use social media." That day is today.

- **The cautious.** You have been using Facebook for some time now and navigate your smartphone expertly, but you'd like to learn more about other social media tools before using them at school. You have seen technology trends come and go, and you want to be sure that you know more than just how to use them; you want to understand why.

- **Early adopter.** You had an invite code to Google+ while it was still in beta. You stood in line at four o'clock in the morning waiting for the latest iOS device. You have the bells and whistles, but the music still doesn't sound very good. You have all of the tools and know how to use them, but you aren't seeing the type of school community engagement you expected. One of your greatest challenges is working with the rest of your faculty, who see you as a tech guru to whom they'll never catch up. This book provides a foundational framework with which your entire team can evaluate and apply social media, no matter what their level of technological proficiency.

- **Noneducator.** The concepts of this book work in situations other than education. The ongoing social engagement model explained in this book is helping professionals from every industry—from entrepreneurs and attorneys to nonprofit leaders and real estate agents—thoughtfully examine the role of social media in their unique context. This book offers specific strategies to help you build community, engage customers, communicate information, and provide value. No matter what your role or your experience with social media, the framework and strategies shared in the following pages will help you engage your community with today's innovative online tools. Now, let's get started!

Introduction

In today's connected world, members of a school community expect more than just open houses and photocopied newsletters. They want frequent updates. They want to give their feedback. They expect to collaborate. School leaders—principals, teachers, and tech specialists—are familiar with social media in their own lives, but because of the complex issues surrounding the use of social media with students they need help effectively using social media in their school practice.

The abundance of social technology has begun to shift the role of the school leader from site administrator to community engagement specialist. Savvy school leaders are responding to this shift by rethinking their leadership strategy, moving from simply communicating to truly connecting.

Exploring tools ranging from Facebook and Twitter to YouTube and Ning, this book walks school leaders step-by-step through a detailed explanation of fourteen of the best online tools available today to engage school communities. Readers will learn to apply the ongoing social engagement model, moving their school community from awareness to advocacy, and from feedback to collaboration. Using screenshots and examples from schools across the country, this book gives readers everything they need to implement social media throughout their campus and community. Whether you work at a private school, a public school, a charter school, or even a university, these social media techniques will help you to engage your target audience and communicate the mission and vision of your school. This book will also serve as another resource in your student recruitment strategy, and inspire business and community involvement.

WHAT IS SOCIAL MEDIA?

Social media involves the use of Web-based technologies to transform one-way communication into an interactive online dialogue. A key component of social media is the creation and exchange of user-generated content. Students and teachers can share original content, enhancing and extending the educational conversations occurring throughout the school community.

A collection of online tools have expanded the definition and capabilities of social media. These tools fall into several major categories:

- **Blogs.** These websites focus on publishing articles according to date or topic and include such platforms as WordPress, Blogger, and Tumblr.

- **Social networks.** These include open networks, such as Facebook; professional sites, such as LinkedIn; and private networks, such as Ning.

- **Microblogs.** Mobile-device-friendly sites allow users to post short updates from any location and to follow other users' posts. Twitter is the dominant tool in this category.

- **eNewsletters.** eNewsletter services allow you to customize e-mail newsletters using form fields, and they include tracking and sharing features. Examples of these tools are Constant Contact and MailChimp.

- **Multimedia hosting sites.** Websites that host pictures as well as audio and video content offer Web users a central place to post their personal and professional media. The most popular tools include YouTube, Flickr, and SoundCloud.

- **Online survey tools.** Many tools have been developed in recent years to allow Web visitors to share their specific feedback. These tools have become more social and flexible, enabling embedding on websites, tracking responses, and integrating data collection into content sharing. These tools include SurveyMonkey and Wufoo.

Recent advances in microblogging and multimedia sharing have enabled an extended conversation, shifting from broadcast to two-way communication, and eventually growing to enable multiple forms of open public discussions. Another recent innovation has been the "like" button, which was made popular by Facebook and which has moved to other platforms, enabling online content to be spread virally from a static website to the extended personal networks of users across the Web. Such sharing, commenting, and creating have led to an online culture of collaboration, a culture in which our students are growing up and that they are expecting in the classroom. Social media has benefits far beyond the classroom, however. It changes and grows the conversations between administrators and teachers, between faculty and parents, and between the school and its surrounding community.

WHY USE SOCIAL MEDIA?

Instead of focusing on the tools, start with the "why." Why use social media at your school? There are many reasons, including families that are more engaged, higher student enrollment, a more collaborative school culture, and stronger community buy-in.

- **Engaged families.** Keep your school community in the loop by sharing events and updates through social media, such as by using Facebook and Twitter. Create greater parent and community awareness of your events. Start communicating information about your events using social media, and you'll see event participation increase. You can also receive feedback via comments through social networks, e-mail entries, and online survey responses. These tools allow you to keep families engaged in a continuous conversation about your school. Families that have a connection with your school will advocate for your school and will aid in your grassroots marketing efforts.

- **Higher student enrollment.** Your Facebook page, Twitter feed, and school website can all work together to engage potential students. Follow up with an eNewsletter and a blog strategy, and you can help ensure that students enroll at your school. Sharing student work through student portfolios will help create ownership and excitement among your current students. Displaying student work in this way also helps you begin a conversation with potential students, offering visitors an inside glimpse into your school and allowing them to make a more informed decision when choosing between your school and another.

- **Collaborative school culture.** Social media connects people's ideas and experiences through flexible technology. A collaborative school culture encourages ongoing engagement; increases awareness of school activities and events; invites feedback on policy decisions; opens conversations over issues both large and small; and empowers members of the community to advocate for the advancement and support of the school, its students, and its staff.

- **Community buy-in.** Social media allows you to build relationships with community members by including them in the conversation, thereby creating more advocates and partners for your organization. Social media gives potential donors a place to hear your story, helping them get to know your school and learn about opportunities to participate.

LEAD THE CONVERSATION

Become a thought leader in your area by frequently using social media. Seeing your school on Facebook and YouTube will add both credibility and personality to your school in the minds of your students, parents, and community members. What you post on your social media pages will have an impact on the conversation taking place at other educational institutions in your area. Creating your own blog and effectively using LinkedIn will also help ensure that the lessons learned at your school will benefit a larger audience.

Your target audience already uses many of the available social media tools. Families are watching online videos for their nightly entertainment. Students use Facebook to stay in touch with their friends. And more and more businesses are discovering the power of Twitter. Using these social media tools can radically influence the community's perception of your school. It also gives you the opportunity to monitor what people are saying about your school and to participate actively in that conversation. This book will show you specific ways to engage the community using the tools that they already use.

BARRIERS TO USING SOCIAL MEDIA

Despite the affordability and capabilities of social media, many school leaders I speak with at conferences and in my consulting work are wary of using social media. Reasons for this include technophobia, school or district policy, and concerns about student safety.

Technophobic Teachers (and School Leaders)

Many educators have admitted to me that they are afraid to try new technology. Reasons they cite include the following:

- It is unreliable.
- It is always changing.
- It takes too much time to learn.
- They might make a mistake.
- They might break something.

School (or District) Policy

Blocking tech tools is common practice. Mobile devices, Twitter, and half of the tools mentioned in this book are frequently banned at schools. Many superintendents, curriculum coordinators, and district technology specialists have taken a strict stance against social networking among students in particular and against social media in general.

Student Safety

Keeping students safe on the Internet is a federal requirement for all schools. Sometimes blocking technology tools just seems easier than trying to use them in a way that actually teaches and protects students. In this book there is an entire chapter focused primarily on student safety, offering specific recommendations for how to address this important issue.

> Steve Hargadon, creator of the Classroom 2.0 social network, writes, "The understandable concerns created by the early and popular networks have overshadowed some amazing changes that are taking place in educational environments when the tools of social networking are being used with students and teachers."
>
> "Social Networking in Education," posted January 11, 2008, www.stevehargadon .com/2008/01/social-networking-in -education.html.

Despite these obvious challenges, social media is here to stay, and the many benefits that social media offers for today's school leaders cannot be ignored. This book shares specific strategies that are working in schools across the country with the goal of inspiring educators to take a second look at social media tools.

FOUNDATIONAL FRAMEWORK FOR SOCIAL MEDIA SUCCESS

The Dixon Ongoing Social Engagement Model stems from ten years of practical experience in digital content creation, personal blogging, and using social media (see Figure I.1). I created this model in response to a need for a foundational framework to help guide school leaders to effectively use developing social media tools, beginning with basic e-mail, leading to blogs, and moving to Facebook. Given the rapid pace at which new social media tools are being developed, I have found this model to assist school leaders in evaluating and using new tools to engage their school community.

The Dixon Ongoing Social Engagement Model is a proven foundational framework to help school leaders better use social media to engage their school community. The stages of the framework are

- **Awareness.** The school tells, the community reads, hears, and sees.
- **Feedback.** The school asks, the community tells.
- **Collaboration.** The school and community work together.
- **Advocacy.** The community promotes and guides the school.

As you continue to use social media to engage your school community, the power and ownership shift from the school distributing content to the school community collaborating on the creation of content. Throughout this book you

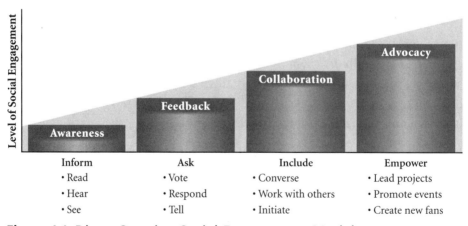

Figure I.1 Dixon Ongoing Social Engagement Model

will learn of tangible ways social media is being used to continually increase the social engagement of school communities following this model.

WHAT TO EXPECT FROM THIS BOOK

This book was written with the practitioner in mind. It's packed with practical examples, scalable strategies, useful tools, and authentic ways to use social media to engage your school community. What began as a guide sharing one school's tips and tricks in using social media has grown into a collection of best practices from school leaders across the country. This book shares practical examples from teachers and principals working in the trenches on a daily basis.

One of the key features of this book is that it offers useful tools that you will be able to use immediately, whether you are a classroom teacher, a school leader, or a leader of many schools. Some of these tools you may have used at your school before. Other tools you may be familiar with, but you may not have experienced their classroom applications. And still other tools will be brand new to you. When a tool is introduced that might be unfamiliar, this book takes the time to explain what the tool is and gives you an overview of its features and benefits. Because social media tools are constantly changing, be sure to visit brianjdixon.com for the latest tips, tricks, and updates.

HOW TO READ THIS BOOK

There are two approaches to reading this book. The first is what most of us do with reference books: we look for a section that is interesting, and we skip right to it. This book is written to support this method of reading, and each chapter is designed to start with the familiar and lead to the unfamiliar topics. If you picked up this book specifically to learn more about Twitter, start with that chapter, but I challenge you also to look at tools you already use, because you may be overlooking key strategies. This includes e-mail, which is a school leader's most underused tool, and the school website, your anchor on the Web that most school leaders do not even know how to update. Chapter Four, School Website, may just change your thinking and empower you to take ownership of your school's public message by better using your website to engage your school community.

The second approach is to read this book from beginning to end. This book in its original form was twice as long. I have painstakingly cut out all unnecessary fat to make this book as practical as possible. Every word, every paragraph, and every example are focused on helping you, the innovative school leader, better use social media to engage your school community and to share your school's story. It is our hope that you read this book all the way through. Skip a section and you may just miss an important idea that could revolutionize your classroom practice.

Finally, social media is a hot topic for school leaders who are looking to use technology effectively to engage and inform their school community. Begin a reading group (or better yet, a Google+ hangout—see Chapter Fourteen) to consider ways that each of you might use the tips shared in this book.

eNewsletters

E-mail newsletters (eNewsletters) are a valuable, cost-effective way to keep your school at the top of your target audience's mind. Having a quick and easy means of communicating with parents, community members, and donors on a regular basis will save you time, money, and trees. An eNewsletter service allows you to use templates; customize content; add social media links; and track views, opens, and forwards. Such services as Constant Contact and MailChimp simplify your eNewsletter strategy with tools for design, contact management, user tracking, eNewsletter archiving, and collecting e-mail addresses. Topics covered in this chapter include

- How eNewsletters work
- Ongoing social engagement with eNewsletters
- Common school tasks before and after eNewsletters

- Best practices for eNewsletters
- Getting started with eNewsletters

HOW ENEWSLETTERS WORK

Although you may be quite familiar with e-mail, you will find that eNewsletters work a bit differently than traditional e-mail. This section outlines six steps in the eNewsletter process, including collecting your contact list, writing the eNewsletter, sending the eNewsletter, tracking interactions, resending the eNewsletter, and archiving content. These steps are followed by a discussion of the advantages posed by eNewsletters over traditional paper-based newsletters.

1. **Collecting your contact list.** Collect the e-mail addresses and contact information of the people with whom you wish to communicate. When writing an eNewsletter, the more information you have about the recipient, the more customized your message can be. At the very least you should collect the first name, last name, e-mail address, and school name of your intended recipients.

2. **Writing the eNewsletter.** The second step when using eNewsletters is to write the content. Approach an eNewsletter more like a traditional newsletter than an e-mail, including short, targeted articles sharing specific information.

3. **Sending the eNewsletter.** Sending an eNewsletter entails a bit more than sending a traditional e-mail. You can schedule your eNewsletter to be sent at a specific time on a specific date. You could write several messages and have them automatically sent out over a few days. You can send one version of the eNewsletter to a subsection of your list, for example parents, and another version to the rest of your list. Some tools, such as MailChimp, even offer intelligent interaction testing; this measures the effectiveness of two versions of an eNewsletter and, after a short testing period, sends out the winning version to the majority of your list.

4. **Tracking interactions.** eNewsletters offer the ability to track recipients' interaction with your message. You'll be able to see which individuals have received the eNewsletter, who opened it, who clicked it, where they clicked, what they did after they clicked, and who forwarded your message.

5. **Resending the eNewsletter.** Based on the tracking features, eNewsletter services allow you to resend the content to your recipients who didn't open your e-mail the first time. As most people today are inundated with a massive number of e-mails, your message may have been lost in their inbox. Often simply sending the e-mail at a more opportune time can drastically increase your response rates. eNewsletter services even help you see when your e-mails are opened, allowing you to better schedule mailings in the future.

6. **Archiving content.** Another great feature of eNewsletters is the ability to archive messages. Your community will be able to read previously sent eNewsletters without your having to post them on your website. An eNewsletter archive can assist you in ensuring that your community has access to any information they may have missed.

eNewsletters feature several key advantages over traditional paper-based newsletters, or compared to standard e-mail programs. These advantages include that they are digital, customizable, and intelligent.

Digital

The first key advantage that eNewsletters have over traditional paper-based newsletters is that they are digital. eNewsletters save time and money by allowing for multiple authors and enabling reusable content. eNewsletters are sent digitally, saving you the cost of paper, copies, and stamps. Because they are scheduled and sent out automatically, you no longer need to worry about adhering address labels, stuffing envelopes, or handing packets out to classes. Multiple users at your school can log in to the eNewsletter service and update their section of the eNewsletter. This can help improve the work flow and ensures that all important information is shared in one single, unified communication from the school. You can also reuse and repurpose previously sent eNewsletters by simply updating the

> *Ron Koehler, president of the National School Public Relations Association, explains, "Consumer needs are changing. The backpack folder is no longer the primary source of information for parents. They want and prefer instant electronic information."*
>
> "National Survey Pinpoints Communication Preferences in School Communication," accessed December 3, 2011, www.nspra .org/files/docs/Release%20on%20CAP%20 Survey.pdf.

content for a new mailing. Reusing sections of prior eNewsletters saves you time and helps to remind the community about upcoming events.

eNewsletter services are also simple to learn and to use. With a wealth of training materials, including screenshot videos, available online, learning how to navigate and use an eNewsletter service is easier than ever. Finally, eNewsletter services even offer mobile applications. For example, Constant Contact has an iPhone application. You can use the app to create and send eNewsletters, track the number of opens and clicks, and access contact information on the go.

Customizable

Another major advantage of eNewsletter services is that they are fully customizable. First, eNewsletter services provide professionally designed templates that you can customize. With simple drag-and-drop features, creating an attractive eNewsletter is effortless. Second, using built-in design tools, you can create beautifully designed, custom eNewsletters in only a few minutes with little computer experience. Adding pictures and changing fonts is very simple with modern eNewsletter tools. You can even embed video content into your eNewsletter to make it particularly engaging. Finally, eNewsletter services allow you to insert form fields that are automatically populated with user data in the final version of the message. For example, you would add the code <first name> to the welcome message, and when the recipient reads the e-mail, it says "Dear Jennifer" or "Dear Matthew." eNewsletters offer a personalized experience, from built-in templates and design tools to the ability to use form fields, far superior to anything that a standard paper-based newsletter could offer.

Intelligent

The greatest advantage of eNewsletters is the data. There is power in understanding who your target audience is, how segments of your audience interact with your eNewsletter, and how your message is being received. You can target each segment of your intended audience by using the contact management features. Start by uploading your e-mail database as a custom list, categorizing your audience segments as parents, students, community volunteers, potential teachers, and so on. Target each group individually with a message that is relevant to them, and choose which list will receive which particular message.

Thanks to interaction tracking, when you send an eNewsletter to your school community you can see how people have interacted with it. With a traditional newsletter, you have no idea what happens to it. Was it read, thrown away, brought home, left in a backpack, or even handed out in class? An eNewsletter service reports data to you, allowing you to see exactly how many people received the eNewsletter, and how many people opened it, clicked it, deleted it, forwarded it, and unsubscribed from it. Understanding how your audience interacts with your eNewsletter is a powerful tool for engaging your school community. eNewsletter services offer intelligent interaction testing, whereby you can simultaneously test two eNewsletters to measure their effectiveness with a small group. The eNewsletter with the most opens or clicks will then be automatically sent out to the rest of the group. This helps ensure that the most effective message reaches the largest audience.

In terms of scheduling, you are able to specify the exact date and time that an eNewsletter is to be delivered. Being able to do this can dramatically increase open rates and click-through rates. From my experience, sending your eNewsletter at Tuesday at 9:00 a.m. and Thursday at 3:00 p.m. seems to yield the highest number of opens. Finally, eNewsletter services offer a customizable sign-up box for your website or blog, allowing your community members to simply add their information and automatically subscribe to your eNewsletter.

ONGOING SOCIAL ENGAGEMENT WITH ENEWSLETTERS

eNewsletters can help build ongoing social engagement online because they increase awareness, allow your school community to easily provide feedback, enable collaboration, and encourage people to advocate for your school (see Figure 1.1).

Awareness

By sending out relevant content about upcoming events, such as parent-teacher night, student showcase night, a sports game, or a school play, you can help build awareness across your school community. Features including an "add to my calendar" button allow your community to take your content and plug it into their existing scheduling system.

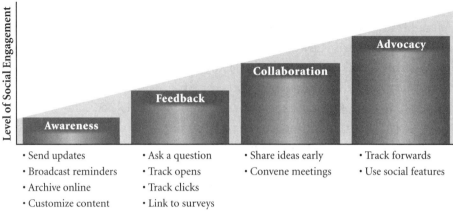

- Send updates
- Broadcast reminders
- Archive online
- Customize content

- Ask a question
- Track opens
- Track clicks
- Link to surveys

- Share ideas early
- Convene meetings

- Track forwards
- Use social features

Figure 1.1 Social Engagement with eNewsletters

Kisu Kuroneko, a seventh- and eighth-grade teacher in Ontario, Canada, explains, "We publish the content of the newsletter as individual posts on the school website. This means that our school community can subscribe to our school website feed and automatically receive updates whenever we add information to the school site."

"WordPress Plug-Ins We Use on Our School Website," posted January 31, 2009, http://blog.classroomteacher.ca/209/wordpress-plugins-we-use-on-our-school-website/#create-an-enewsletter-for-your-school.

Feedback

eNewsletters also allow for feedback from your audience. When you ask a question in your eNewsletter, there are several ways to receive feedback. You could have a vote, asking a simple yes-no question. Readers click one link for "yes" or another link for "no." You can track the number of clicks to see how many people agreed and how many people disagreed. You can have a link to a comment box, in which readers post a comment to send to you. You can also integrate an online survey platform, enabling readers to give authentic feedback.

Collaboration

eNewsletters provide an opportunity for collaboration with your school community. By sending out information or polling your community, you are inviting them to get involved by sending their feedback and their ideas. Allow this feedback to be the beginning of a conversation. Use your eNewsletter to keep parents engaged in that conversation by sharing progress on putting their ideas into action.

Advocacy

eNewsletters are a great tool to help facilitate advocacy in your school community and to help you empower your school to advocate for your cause. One method of doing this is to track forwards. This will enable you to see how people are sharing your content with their contacts. Many eNewsletter services also include social features, including Facebook and Twitter links, that allow your community to share the eNewsletter with their social media followers with just a few clicks.

COMMON SCHOOL TASKS BEFORE AND AFTER ENEWSLETTERS

Using eNewsletters can change the way you complete common school tasks. These include easily sending weekly newsletters, receiving targeted responses, and communicating information to specific groups.

Task or Goal	Traditional Method	Using eNewsletters
Sending weekly newsletters	Everyone would receive newsletters in the form of paper photocopies, which were handed out physically.	eNewsletters are automatically sent via an online program. You can track views and send the eNewsletter to a targeted list.
Receiving targeted responses	You would call individuals representative of a target demographic. Alternately, a specific group would be called for a meeting in which they were asked for their feedback in person.	The eNewsletter list can be segmented to enable communication specific to a target demographic. You can then track views and clicks from the targeted eNewsletter segment.
Communicating information to specific groups	You would host a special meeting to share information, or you might make personal phone calls to a targeted list.	The eNewsletter list is segmented to communicate to specific groups.

BEST PRACTICES FOR ENEWSLETTERS

Fully taking advantage of the dynamic features of eNewsletters involves implementing some best practices. These include writing relevant content, avoiding spam, and capturing e-mail addresses.

Writing Relevant Content

eNewsletters must provide valid content that the reader will want to read. Otherwise you will see low open rates and an increase in the number of readers unsubscribing. eNewsletters do not have to be stodgy, formal documents. They can be fun and lively. Consider including surprising facts about your faculty; notifications of recent awards and student achievements; reminders about interesting events happening at the school and in the area; historical information about your school; games, contests, quizzes, and trivia; and inspirational quotes.

According to Roberta Furger, contributing writer for Edutopia, "E-Newsletters skip the middleman and send the information directly to parents' e-mail accounts. They're quick, cheap, and reliable."

"How to Boost Parental Involvement," posted August 10, 2009, www.edutopia.org/parent-involvement-participation-education-tips.

Remember that your eNewsletter is often viewed in an overflowing e-mail inbox. You have a short amount of time to get and keep the attention of your reader. Understanding some basic strategies that can increase your recipients' engagement with your eNewsletter will benefit your school by ensuring higher open and click-through rates.

- **Have a compelling e-mail subject line.** One way to help your eNewsletter stand out is to write a compelling subject line. Try using such phrases as "important news about your child" or "we need your feedback by Thursday." These subject lines inspire action.

- **Use pictures.** Use the first section of your eNewsletter to grab your audience's attention with relevant pictures and other visual elements.

- **Don't bury the headline.** Share the most important information first. If one of your articles in the eNewsletter focuses on the parent open house night, start with that information: "parent open house night on Thursday." Ensure that your content is "scannable," allowing readers to glance through the eNewsletter and quickly read the most important content.

- **Offer value.** Think about your content from the perspective of your readers, and consider how you can offer something of value to them. Go beyond just sharing information; provide clear strategies to assist your readers with the problems they face.

- **Call readers to action.** Every e-mail should include an invitation to respond or take action. Providing a method for readers to respond to your content, such as an RSVP link, survey question, or short quiz, will increase their feedback and engagement.

Avoiding Spam

One key when writing your eNewsletter is to avoid spam. The term *spam* refers to the percentage of e-mail messages you have sent that recipients have marked as unsolicited. To avoid sending spam, make sure that every recipient of your eNewsletter has given you permission to send e-mail to him or her. Ensuring your eNewsletter list is "permission based" also helps guarantee that your message will be delivered to the recipient's e-mail inbox. Not only is unsolicited e-mail not read but also your eNewsletter service might block your account. There may even be strict fines imposed on people who send a large amount of unsolicited e-mail. You can avoid this by making sure that your school community has given you permission to send eNewsletters to their e-mail addresses.

Capturing E-Mail Addresses

Ensure that every visitor to your website is invited to sign up for your eNewsletter. Collecting e-mail addresses allows your school to continue the conversation with visitors once they have left your site. There are several methods for capturing new e-mail sign-ups.

- **Registration forms.** When a new student signs up for your school, or when parents sign up as volunteers, include a space on the registration form for e-mail addresses. Make sure that the space in which the e-mail address is written has a single cell for each character. E-mail addresses must be written legibly for someone to receive your e-mail. One mistake—a period or a "0" instead of an "o"—means that the intended recipient will not get your message. Below the e-mail entry box, write a disclaimer: "By entering your e-mail address, you will be added to our school eNewsletter."

- **Contests.** Another way to collect e-mail addresses from parents is to have a contest. Have parents place their business card in a fish bowl for a prize drawing at a parent event. It must be stated near the fishbowl: "By entering your business card, you will be added to our eNewsletter list to receive information about our school and notices of school events. If you would not like to receive this eNewsletter, please write 'no list' on the back of your business card."

- **Phone calls.** When parents call your school to find out more information or to check in on their child, personally invite them to subscribe to your eNewsletter. Empower your front office staff to ask parents about the latest eNewsletter. Ensure that your receptionist is asking parents, "Did you receive our eNewsletter on Thursday?" For every parent who says no (and there will be a lot), the follow-up response is, "Let me write down your e-mail address to make sure we have the right one." In that context, it's very difficult to turn the receptionist down. He or she will record the e-mail address and add it to the database immediately.

- **E-mail signatures.** Make sure that all of your faculty members have "To subscribe to your school eNewsletter, click here" in their e-mail signature. This will help spread awareness about your school eNewsletter, and increase the number of people signing up for it.

GETTING STARTED WITH ENEWSLETTERS

Question for Reflection: Track how many pieces of paper your school sends home in the course of a week. How might this same information be shared more intelligently with an eNewsletter?

First Steps

1. Consider how you might personalize a message you traditionally send to a group. Start with your teachers by adding their first name using a form field in your eNewsletter service. For example: "Alicia, I wanted to remind you about the faculty meeting on Thursday."

2. Scan through your old e-mails to find any eNewsletters you have received from other schools or businesses. Read these over to discover what techniques capture your attention.

Facebook

This chapter offers a thorough explanation of Facebook, the world's most popular social networking site, along with the many opportunities and challenges of using social networking in school communities. A Facebook page can serve as a central place for relating story information and for bringing a school's community members together. This chapter shares best practices for using Facebook to increase social engagement. Topics covered include

- What is Facebook?
- How Facebook works
- Ways to connect on Facebook
- Benefits of Facebook
- Ongoing social engagement with Facebook

- Common school tasks before and after Facebook
- Advertising on Facebook
- Privacy and safety concerns on Facebook
- Tech-savvy Facebook
- Getting started with Facebook

WHAT IS FACEBOOK?

Facebook is the world's most popular social networking site. On Facebook, users create personal profiles and connect to their friends by sharing photos, links, and updates. Facebook was originally started to help college students get to know each other by sharing information about themselves online. Although Facebook was once only available to students, it is now open to the entire world, allowing people to connect with anyone worldwide. Today there are more than five hundred million active Facebook users, and 50 percent of those users log on to Facebook in any given day.

To keep your school community engaged, you must maintain a presence on Facebook. The old real estate adage is true: it's all about location, location, location. To communicate with students, parents, and the local community, go where the people are. Facebook is the new town hall, the new civic center, the new hub of community activity—which is exactly where your school needs to be. Because members of your school community are already using Facebook, your school's Facebook page can serve as an essential gathering place of information and can host a central conversation about your school.

HOW FACEBOOK WORKS

For those who have never used Facebook, there are essentially three steps to getting started with your personal account (Facebook pages for schools will be covered later in this chapter). First create your profile, next add your friends, and then communicate with your friends.

1. **Create your profile.** On Facebook, you create an account using your real name and information to describe yourself, including where you live, your hobbies and interests, the places you've worked, the schools you've

attended, and other personal information. All of this information is placed onto your online profile, helping others find you on Facebook and allowing friends to get to know you better.

2. **Add your friends.** Once you complete your personal Facebook profile, you can begin to "friend" other Facebook users. Friending is the process of locating people on Facebook whom you know, requesting that they confirm they know you, and viewing and commenting on their Facebook profile. Once you connect with someone on Facebook, his or her updates and posts will appear on your newsfeed. The newsfeed is the first page you see when you log on to Facebook, and it is continually updated with content that your friends have recently posted. This constantly changing source of news and updates is the main reason why many Facebook users log on almost every day. They want to see the latest photos, updates, and links from their friends. This ongoing interaction among friends through viewing posts, responding to comments, and tagging photos is why Facebook is known as a social network. You can interact with all of your friends on one easy-to-use site.

3. **Communicate with your friends.** Once you are connected to friends on Facebook, there are several ways to communicate with them. First, all of your friends will be able to see any updates that you post on your profile. They can comment on your posts or click the "like" button if they respond positively to what you have posted. Second, you can post a comment on a friend's Facebook wall. The Facebook wall is a public place that can be updated by you and your friends. Third, you can automatically invite friends to events by adding their name to the guest list in Facebook Events. Finally, you can send a direct message to a specific person, similar to an e-mail, that can only be viewed by that individual in his or her Facebook inbox.

WAYS TO CONNECT ON FACEBOOK

Facebook not only connects you to people you know but also allows you to stay connected to schools, causes, and affinity groups. The tools for connecting in this way include Facebook pages, Facebook groups, and Facebook events.

Facebook Pages

Instead of creating personal Facebook profiles, schools are able to create Facebook pages. Unlike a Facebook profile, which has a variety of privacy settings, a Facebook page is publicly viewable by all users on Facebook. Your school's Facebook page serves as a central place for you and your community to share and update information about your school, to post comments, and to upload photos. When someone clicks the "like" button on a Facebook page, updates from that page are included in that user's newsfeed. In this way, users can see the latest updates, photos, and links from your school without ever having to visit your page. In other words, maintaining your Facebook page is an ongoing way to keep your community updated on your school in a place they regularly visit.

Elements of a Facebook Page

A Facebook page contains the following elements, with the numbers in this list matching the numbers in the sample Facebook page shown in Figure 2.1:

1. **Profile icon.** This should be a photo that is easily connected to your school, such as your school logo or mascot.

2. **School name.** Your full school name goes here.

3. **"About" section.** You only have a few sentences to describe your school in this section, so focus on the most important keywords.

4. **Contact information.** Your school address, phone number, and office hours go here.

5. **Sharing feature.** This is where you enter new posts, upload photos and videos, share links, and add new events. Anything you would like your target audience to know should be placed here.

6. **Recent updates.** This section of your Facebook page's wall features recent updates including events, links, and photos.

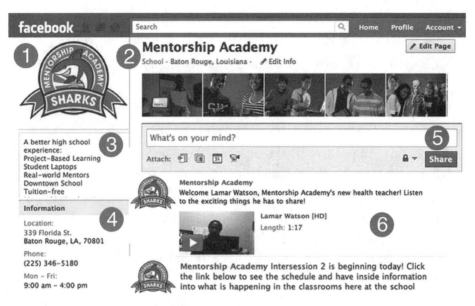

Figure 2.1 Screenshot: Facebook Page

Keys to a Dynamic Facebook Page

Keep your school community engaged by following these best practices: post new content at least once per day, keep your school Facebook page fun and positive, share relevant information about your school, and upload multimedia content to engage viewers.

- **Post new content every day.** By updating your page at least twice a day, you engage your fans in a daily conversation. Here are some ideas for content you can post:

  - *Student reminders*—"Senior ski trip permission forms are due to Mr. Harris by 10:00 a.m. on Thursday."

Peter Kupfer, a physics teacher from Lake Zurich, Illinois, has had much success with his classroom's Facebook page. "Within a month of creating a Facebook fan page, 60 percent of my students had become fans, and 75 percent said the page reminded them at least once that they had homework. Finally, I was communicating with students 'in their world' and helping them be successful in class."

"Social Matter," posted January 5, 2011, www.edtechmagazine.com/k12/article/2011/01/social-matter.

- *Celebrations of students*—"Congratulations to Katrina Boronow for winning the regional spelling bee. Her winning word was *prolegomenous*."

- *Class announcements*—"Mrs. Anderson's students are presenting their environmental science projects today at 11:00 a.m. in the auditorium."

- *Event postings*—"The next school board meeting will be Tuesday, October 15th, at 4:00 p.m. in the library conference room."

- **Keep it fun and positive.** By keeping your page fun and positive, your school will benefit from the casual familiarity that people experience on Facebook.

- **Share relevant information.** Consider what your community wants to know about your school. Relevant information, including event reminders, links to forms, or updates on schedules (such as notices of half days, parent conferences, and games) will ensure that parents and students find value in the content you post.

- **Upload multimedia content.** Photos and videos are a powerful means of engaging your school community. Posting photos, videos, and links keeps your community members updated on the latest news at your school and encourages them to visit your page frequently. Everyone wants to see pictures and videos of themselves and their friends.

> Shawn Roner, a high school principal in San Diego, explains, "One of the most powerful ways school administrators can use Facebook is to provide parents with a unique inside view of the daily operations of the school. Administrators can take pictures of daily events, record interviews with teachers and students, film student projects or particular parts of a teacher's lesson and share this information with parents."
>
> "Using Facebook to Improve School Communication," posted November 24, 2009, http://edbuzz.org/sroner/2009/11/using-facebook-to-improve-school-communication/.

Facebook Groups

Facebook groups provide a closed space for small groups of users to communicate about shared interests. Groups enable collaboration through such features as discussions, group messages, shared calendars, and group documents. Because groups are not publicly viewable and are by invitation or request only, they can be used effectively for sports teams, school clubs, committees, and parent associations, and as a vehicle for teacher collaboration.

Facebook Events

Schools can take advantage of the Facebook Events feature to help manage the logistics of the events they host. This is much more effective than just posting event information on your website and hoping people attend. Facebook Events allows you to

1. **Invite the community.** Create a Facebook event with all of the necessary details, such as the time, place, and cost. Post a link to the event on your school's Facebook page, and send an invitation to members of your school community.

2. **Manage attendance.** Recipients of your invitation will respond to the event invitation by RSVP'ing "yes," "no," or "maybe." You'll be able to view how many people are coming to your event through the Facebook Events feature.

3. **Post updates.** Keep attendees engaged and excited about your event by posting reminders through Facebook Events. Attendees will be notified of any changes made to events via e-mail and through Facebook notifications.

BENEFITS OF FACEBOOK

There are many reasons to use Facebook as part of your school's social engagement strategy. Facebook is easy to use, accessible, ubiquitous, and manageable.

- **Easy to use.** Facebook is surprisingly simple. There are built-in tools to upload e-mail contacts. The "people you may know" feature suggests friends based on your existing contacts, simplifying the process of connecting to people. It's quick and easy to stay updated on your friends' activities online by viewing your newsfeed. Posting content is now easier than ever with Facebook Connect, a feature that allows you to log on to other websites using your Facebook username and password.

- **Accessible.** Another advantage of Facebook is its accessibility. Your community members are able to view the site on a computer, using an application on their phone, or from other Internet-connected devices. Facebook limits the use of pop-ups and other Web gimmicks, making it a stable platform for your content. Posting your content on Facebook helps ensure that members of your school community will be able to access the most current information from wherever they are.

- **Ubiquitous.** A third advantage of Facebook is its ubiquity. Of all people who have Internet access, 40 percent use Facebook. This increases to 70 percent when limited to students. Such widespread adoption of Facebook makes it an ideal tool for engaging your community. For example, Facebook allows you to connect to your school's alumni. When users sign up, one of the profile questions asks them about their educational experience. After you have created your school's Facebook page, alumni will be able to link to your page. They'll probably be interested in current happenings at their former school. Connecting to alumni can help your fundraising and mentoring efforts. This is just one example of how Facebook's ubiquity helps you connect to your school's key stakeholders.

- **Manageable.** You can make multiple users administrators on your school's Facebook page. Having a few reliable staff members regularly update your school Facebook page ensures that content is unique and frequently updated. You can even manage your personal profile and your school's Facebook page from one user account without having to log out as yourself and log in as your school. Consider making a few students "media ambassadors" who are tasked with deleting inappropriate posts, responding to comments, and removing users from your Facebook page. This could be a great role for a few tech-savvy students who are interested in contributing to the school community.

ONGOING SOCIAL ENGAGEMENT WITH FACEBOOK

Facebook is a dynamic tool for increasing your school's ongoing social engagement (see Figure 2.2). Facebook allows you to build awareness, receive feedback, collaborate with your school community, and empower your fans to advocate for your school.

Awareness

Facebook allows you to spread awareness about your school by posting updates, pictures, and links on your Facebook page. You can also use Facebook as a

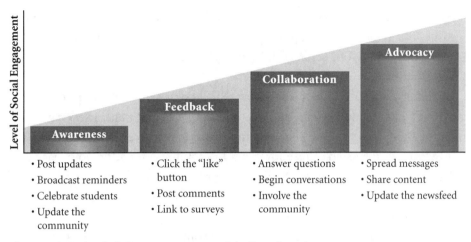

Figure 2.2 Social Engagement with Facebook

platform to build awareness of your school's mission and vision. Ongoing communication might involve posting information on programs or activities reflective of your school's mission and vision, or posting media files of meetings that relate to that mission and vision.

Feedback

Facebook is a dynamic social media tool for receiving feedback from your school community. For example, the "like" button allows your friends or fans of your Facebook page to provide instant feedback. For example, our school recently posted a picture of our new mascot on our Facebook page. When students clicked the "like" button, this action was then posted both on our school's Facebook page and on their newsfeed, allowing all of their Facebook friends to see that they liked the mascot picture. This spread awareness of our new mascot to an exponentially

Salem School District in Oregon attracts responses from community members on its Facebook posts, explains Kimberly Melton, a reporter at the Oregonian. *To do this they "solicited suggestions to name a new district program that brings people in to spend a day as a student, staff member or principal. Some of the responses: 'A day in the life of . . . ,' 'So you want to be a . . . ,' and 'Where in the world is . . .'"*

"Schools Use Facebook, Twitter to Get Out Their Message," posted September 24, 2009, www.oregonlive.com/education/index.ssf/2009 /09/schools_turn_to_facebook_twitt.html.

larger group of people than would have seen it if it had only been posted on our website. Facebook "pushes" updates out to your followers so that they can "stay in the loop" about your school while they are checking in on their friends' and family's activity.

Another way to receive feedback on Facebook is through user comments. Anytime you post something on your school's Facebook page, users can comment on that post. As the Facebook administrator, you receive an e-mail when a new comment is posted. This allows you to monitor content on your page and delete inappropriate comments before they are seen by too many members of your school community. You can also respond to comments and answer questions posted by community members.

A final way to receive feedback from your community on Facebook is to post a link to a survey. Using an online survey tool, such as SurveyMonkey or Wufoo, you can track click-through rates, obtain user feedback, and perform sophisticated statistical analysis. Surveying your school community can provide insights into issues or interests of which you may not be aware.

Steve Johnson, a middle school technology facilitator in North Carolina, believes that social networking sites such as Facebook allow parents and students to collaborate, connect, and learn together. He states, "Society is moving toward a model of shared knowledge building, where people from all over the world can interact, question, reflect, and reshape thinking in meaningful ways."

"Making the Case for Social Media in Education," posted March 11, 2010, www .edutopia.org/social-media-case-education -edchat-steve-johnson.

Collaboration

Facebook is a great tool for beginning conversations to increase the level of collaboration you have with your school community. Allowing multiple users to post their own ideas and content in a public place shifts user control from a single administrative team to a collaborative school, thus enabling community members to initiate ideas and programs.

Advocacy

The social features of Facebook make it the perfect tool for having your fans advocate for your school. Perhaps the most dynamic tool on Facebook is the sharing feature. You can harness the power of crowds and social networks to take your school's updates and your content and share them with a much larger community than the one to which you would have access on your own.

For example, if your school were hosting a teacher hiring fair, traditionally you might post a notice in a public place, such as the district office; you might send an e-mail to people you know; and you would post the announcement on your school website. With Facebook, however, you can harness the power of other people's social networks to spread awareness of the teacher hiring fair, simply by posting on your wall. When fans "like" or comment on your post, their respective social networks see that post, helping your message spread further into networks to which you do not have access. School leaders can effectively build their school community by encouraging students to post positive feedback on Facebook.

COMMON SCHOOL TASKS BEFORE AND AFTER FACEBOOK

Many common school tasks are easier with Facebook. For example, let's say the Robotics Team at your school wants to accomplish a number of goals, including raising money to travel to and participate in the National Robotics Tournament. The table compares traditional methods used to accomplish these tasks to the social engagement that is possible through Facebook.

Teacher Heather Wolpert-Gawron, an award-winning middle school teacher and staff blogger for Edutopia, finds that Facebook is a place for advocacy among teachers, parents, and colleagues. "Facebook was more than just a means to learn about friends professionally and colleagues personally: It became a way to publicize the issues each of us felt deserved advocacy."

"Social Media in Education: The Power of Facebook," posted May 7, 2010, www .edutopia.org/social-media-education -examples-facebook.

The Bloomington High School wrestling team in California has over a thousand likes. They take advantage of the Facebook sharing feature to spread news of wrestling events through social media into the wider community. Their page proclaims: "The #1 followed high school wrestling face book page in Southern California."

"Bloomington High School Wrestling," accessed December 3, 2011, www.facebook .com/pages/Bloomington-High-School -Wrestling/131135440235156?sk=info.

Task or Goal	Traditional Method	Using Facebook
Recruiting students to be on the Robotics Team	A photocopied or hand-painted poster board would be hung in the school's hallway. Members of the team might invite new students to participate by personally asking them between classes or on the phone.	A video from the robotics teacher that showcases the team's robot could be posted on the school's Facebook page to be seen by its fans, including parents and community members. Each time a user likes the video, this invitation to join the club spreads further across that user's social network and is seen by more people. The video links to an online sign-up form for interested students. There is also an invitation to join the Robotics Team group on Facebook to stay updated. The video and link are quickly spread to other students.
Fundraising for materials	Traditionally the Robotics Team's fundraisers would include hosting bake sales at the school, asking for donations from local businesses, and asking friends and family members to give a small monetary donation.	The Robotics Team can help spread the message of their fundraising goal much more widely through Facebook than by word of mouth. There are, in fact, many fundraising tools that integrate with Facebook, including PayPal and DonorsChoose.org.
Promoting local tournaments	Promoting local tournaments at your school might happen in the form of a poster in the school hallway, verbal announcements on the school's intercom, and word of mouth.	Using the Facebook Events feature, the Robotics Team can track attendees and notify them when news about the tournament changes.

Task or Goal	Traditional Method	Using Facebook
Selling T-shirts	The team would take preorders from the school community, with sizes, and pay the local set-up fee to print an additional ten to twenty T-shirts. They would sell them at school and deliver them in person.	The team can take advantage of print-on-demand technology to allow fans to buy multiple versions of the robotics T-shirt using Zazzle. The team can create its own virtual store and post a link to it on Facebook. This way, the team doesn't spend any money on their T-shirts, they can offer multiple designs to increase interest, and they easily receive a portion of the revenue.
Announcing tournament results	After winning a big tournament, the Robotics Team would be celebrated on the morning announcements, and a trophy would be placed in the school's trophy case.	Using Facebook, members of the Robotics Team can update their status to reflect their big tournament win. They can also record, edit, and upload a video highlight reel of the tournament. On the school's Facebook page, Robotics Team members are able to post links to media coverage and photo albums of the event. This allows other members of the community to experience the triumph of the Robotics Team's victory.
Fundraising for the national tournament	Students would raise money and have to pay a large fee for the national tournament.	Using the power of Facebook, the team can set a fundraising goal and engage the community to track and reach that goal.
Hosting the year-end banquet	The Robotics Team might host a year-end banquet at the local country club, and each member would pay out of pocket for his or her place setting.	Using Facebook, members of the Robotics Team are able to engage the larger community to sponsor the year-end banquet. This sponsorship helps them host the banquet for free in exchange for recognition of the local companies. During the banquet, program highlights from the year in the form of status updates, quotes, and pictures are displayed on the screen for all to experience.

ADVERTISING ON FACEBOOK

Depending on your marketing budget, Facebook ads can be an effective tool for recruiting students, recruiting teachers, and engaging the community. Facebook ads allow you to target specific demographics, therefore building your reputation with those particular audience segments. For just a few dollars, you can create an ad campaign on Facebook to target a specific subset of users.

A Facebook ad appears on the right side of users' profiles, walls, and activity pages, allowing them to click on the ad. Destinations include a website, or the organization's Facebook page. The advantage of Facebook ads is that the users are already on Facebook, so you have their attention. When someone likes an organization, he or she will receive status updates from that organization.

Brittany Fishman, an admissions associate for the American Hebrew Academy, states, "I find updating the Facebook page to be one of the most rewarding parts of my day. Because we are a boarding school, the page allows parents to stay connected with school happenings and see pictures of their kids involved with schoolwork and extracurriculars. It also serves us well as a channel of student recruitment and general PR."

"How Schools Can Use Facebook to Build an Online Community" (in comments), accessed December 3, 2011, http://mashable.com/2011 /04/26/facebook-for-schools/.

Creating a Facebook Ad

Here are five components your Facebook ad should have to recruit new students and stakeholders:

1. **Title.** Write a clear, attention-grabbing title. Be specific about what you are offering, or you will end up paying for clicks by visitors who aren't part of your target audience.

2. **Body text.** Now that you have the viewers' attention, you have just a few words to convince them to click. Use your keywords here and include a "call to action" to ensure that they click for more information. We use action phrases like "learn movie making," "build robots," and "visit us" to entice visitors to click on our ad to learn more about our school.

3. **Image.** You only have a small picture to get your audience's attention. Instead of including a logo or picture of the school, we used a stock photo of a student who's filming a movie. The picture is the first element of your

ad that visitors will notice, so balance grabbing their attention with including a photo that best relates to them and represents your school.

4. **Destination URL.** This is the link to the landing page to which visitors are led after they click on your ad.

5. **Landing page.** This can be a page with a video, your website, or a form to collect their e-mail addresses and add them to your eNewsletter list. Viewers who clicked on our ad were directed to a landing page on which they watched an overview video about our school and could sign up for our eNewsletter.

Targeting Your Ad

Facebook allows you to be very selective about who sees your ad, ensuring that you only pay to advertise to members of your target audience. You can narrowly focus your ad based on data ranging from geographic location and age to likes and interests.

Measuring Return on Investment of Facebook Ads

To serve as an example, here are a few statistics from an ad we ran to recruit students over a twenty-four-hour period:

- **Impressions.** Impressions are the number of times that our ad was displayed on the screen to members of our target audience. On July 1st our ad was displayed 241,622 times. This is the number of times the ad appeared on a page, whether or not viewers noticed it. The clicks are what count.

- **Social percentage.** Facebook ads display the names of your school's fans who have clicked on an ad to help encourage their friends to also click on the ad. This "social percentage" shows the impact growing your fan base can have on engaging new fans. The more fans you have, the more people who vouch for your content through clicks, the more you can reach new fans. Our social percentage was 58.2 percent. This means that over half of our ad clicks were tied to a social connection, increasing the trust factor.

- **Clicks.** Clicks are counted each time a user clicks through your ad to your landing page. Our ad was clicked 93 times on July 1st. This number is the key to measuring the ad's effectiveness.

- **Click-through rate (CTR).** The click-through rate (CTR) is the number of clicks your ad receives divided by the number of times your ad is shown on the site (impressions) in the same time period. Our CTR was .04 percent, meaning that a small fraction of people who saw the ad clicked on it.

- **Average cost per click (CPC).** In this example, we used the cost-per-click model. Using this model, you are only charged when your ad is clicked on, allowing you to pay for audience engagement, not for content broadcasting. Our CPC was $0.52, meaning that it cost about half a dollar to reach each person who clicked on our ad.

- **Amount spent.** This is the total amount we spent for one day of advertising on Facebook. For $48.34, our ad appeared 241,622 times and was clicked on 93 times. Although we also used traditional media, such as the local news, student recruitment events, face-to-face presentations, billboards, and post-cards, the best use of our school's money was Facebook ads. The average billboard costs $1,000 a month. Imagine how much further these dollars could go with a specifically targeted Facebook ad campaign.

PRIVACY AND SAFETY CONCERNS ON FACEBOOK

Facebook can be a dynamic tool for whole-school communication. Few schools have ventured to allow the use of Facebook during the school day on the school network. If that is something you are considering, be sure to thoroughly review the privacy and safety concerns outlined here:

- **Cyberbullying.** Experiencing negative comments or some form of bullying online is common for many teens today. What was once a note passed in class or a negative comment in the locker room is now a series of demeaning comments made public on social networks. School administrators must ensure that any instance of cyberbullying is addressed so that it does not continue to spread or lead to offline physical or verbal bullying.

- **Privacy issues.** Nothing you do on a computer today is private. Anyone who has had a computer hacked or stolen knows that once something is typed on a computer or sent over the Internet there are ways for that information to get out. If you work at a public school, there are legalities surrounding what you send and post using a state-owned computer. Although Facebook does offer privacy features, once others view your profile, you never know what they are going to do with that information—print it, save it, edit it, photocopy it, or forward it via e-mail. Privacy is in many ways a thing of the past when it comes to the Internet.

- **Inappropriate staff-student relationships.** There is much debate as to whether teachers should be friends with their students on Facebook. Several states actually have laws banning the practice. Two concerns school leaders should have when staff members communicate with students on Facebook are the appropriateness and transparency of their interaction. Although Facebook can improve communication and extend students' access to their teachers beyond the school day, dialogue in social networks can quickly turn from beneficial to inappropriate when unmonitored.

Given these safety concerns, embracing Facebook as a tool for social engagement requires schools to implement specific safety strategies. By establishing a clear user policy, by offering parents and students training, and by monitoring student activity on Facebook, school leaders can keep students safe online.

Clear User Policy

To help manage students' use of Facebook, establish a clear user policy. Schools usually have an Acceptable Use Policy for students that is written in "legalese." Make it clear to students and their parents what the consequences will be if a student's Facebook post has a negative impact on the school community. Make it clear in the faculty handbook whether or not teachers and students can be friends on Facebook. I would personally recommend against it. Instead, I suggest that students and teachers collaborate online using professional networking sites; these include Ning, Google Sites, and Moodle.

Parent Training

Bring in an expert who can speak to parents about Internet safety at home and at school. Hosting a "parent university" night is a creative way to educate parents on a difficult topic.

Student Training

Teens need to learn how to use social media effectively. Schools that implement an online collaborative network help prepare students to appropriately use social media tools outside of school. Students should receive ongoing training in staying safe online, learning the following key points:

- What you post is never private; it can be printed, screen captured, forwarded, and saved.
- What you post cannot be erased; it is permanent.
- Your online activity reflects your offline reality.

Monitoring Student Activity Online

To help combat cyberbullying, consider monitoring student activity on Facebook. Privacy settings on Facebook profiles make it difficult for school leaders to see negative comments posted by students, but there are still ways to monitor students' Facebook accounts. First, you can empower a group of students to be your school's online safety monitors. When dramatic situations, such as bullying or threats of a fight, are posted on Facebook, these students report the threat to school officials, who are able to contact parents and handle the situation immediately. A second way to monitor student activity online is to create a personal Facebook account to friend students on Facebook. There are two ways to do this:

- **Create a Facebook profile for the school mascot.** A Facebook profile is a personal Facebook account of an individual person. To view users' profiles, you'll need to be friends with them on Facebook. One way school leaders have done this is by creating a personal account as their school mascot. We created a Facebook profile for Megabyte, the Mentorship Academy mascot. Megabyte's account is able to friend students, and because Megabyte isn't an authority figure students are likely to accept his friend requests. All administrators have access to the Megabyte account and can use this account when researching incidents that inevitably occur on Facebook.

- **Use your own personal Facebook account.** A second way to see student activity on Facebook is using a personal Facebook account. Some school administrators have blurred the line between school life and home life and have made their personal Facebook account open to their school community.

I only recommend this tactic for school administrators and not for classroom teachers, as administrators are the key staff addressing parents and schoolwide discipline issues. It is important to be able to research bullying that occurs online, especially when it affects your school community. By being Facebook friends with students and parents, you can see what they've posted on Facebook. Becoming aware of what students already know can help you be more "in tune" with issues that have an impact on your school community.

TECH-SAVVY FACEBOOK

This section features innovative ideas and next-level projects for those who have mastered the basics of this social media tool.

iFrames

Working with your school's technology coordinator, you can embed a scaled-down version of your school website into your Facebook page using the iFrames feature. Embedding an iFrame into your Facebook page gives users a more dynamic online experience by providing links, videos, and sign-up forms. Instead of having to send users to a separate website, you can let them fill out information right on your Facebook page. There are a few advantages to using this iFrame feature. First, it is more convenient for the user to access one page through Facebook. Second, there is a level of trust using Facebook that there might not be when using the school's official website. Third, using Facebook ensures that the embedded website will be properly formatted for viewing on multiple devices, unlike with many Flash-based school websites. Although creating an iFrame on your Facebook page may require some assistance from a Web developer, it may be worth investigating.

Check-Ins

Another advanced feature is Facebook Places. Facebook Places allows you to "check in" to your favorite physical locations from the Facebook application on your mobile device. By checking in, you are notifying your friends in real time of exactly where you are. Although many users have privacy concerns in regard to Facebook Places, using this type of location-based application is a growing trend among tech-savvy Facebook users, particularly students.

Schools can use the Facebook Places feature in several ways. You can make your school a "place" on Facebook, allowing visitors to check in at your school online. All of the content uploaded at your school, including photos, videos, and comments, will be tagged with your school's location. Another way to use Facebook Places is to have your school mascot check in at different locations around town. When your sports teams play against other schools, for example, your mascot could check in at the rival school. A third way to use Facebook Places as a school is within the classroom. Location-based tools such as Facebook Places allow for some fascinating integrations between technology and classroom content, such as orienteering, civics, and geography. As the features of mobile devices continue to improve, innovative teachers will use this technology to advance opportunities for authentic learning.

GETTING STARTED WITH FACEBOOK

Question for Reflection: Based on the suggestions in this chapter, how might you better manage your school's social media presence?

First Steps

1. If you haven't already, sign up for Facebook for your own personal use. Beginning to use this tool in your personal life will help you discover its educational applications.

2. Reach out to a local Internet safety nonprofit to schedule a parent workshop.

CHAPTER

3

Twitter

In this chapter we will review the process of integrating Twitter into your schoolwide communication strategy. From building awareness through announcements and reminders to increasing feedback and collaboration using @ replies and #keywords, you can use Twitter as a dynamic tool for building social engagement throughout the school community. Topics include

- How Twitter works
- Learning the Twitter lingo
- Twitter features
- Ongoing social engagement with Twitter
- Common school tasks before and after Twitter
- Best practices for using Twitter
- Getting started with Twitter

HOW TWITTER WORKS

Twitter is a microblogging messaging service that limits you to 140 characters per message, including spaces and punctuation, to post updated content. Twitter began by asking the question, "What are you doing now?" Essentially, it is an instant messaging service for the masses, allowing users to post updates anytime from anywhere to be read by anyone.

Newcomers to social media sometimes get Twitter and Facebook mixed up. They are often used in the same sentence, but they are very different. Twitter is primarily a mobile platform. You can follow people, but they don't have to follow you back. Likewise, people can follow you, but you don't have to follow them back. Facebook, by contrast, can serve as your central hub of social activity, allowing you to create a profile, send pictures and videos, see what your friends are doing, view content and read articles, and organize your social life. Twitter primarily involves updating your status and sharing content. In fact, Twitter and Facebook can work together. You can post an update on Twitter and have it automatically posted as a status update on Facebook, and vice versa.

Twitter allows you to post status updates, called "tweets," to answer the simple question, "What are you doing now?" Schools always have news and events in which the larger community would be interested, and Twitter is a great tool for sharing this information with tech-savvy community members.

Reading Tweets

On Twitter, you can read the updates of anyone who uses the service, from the latest news to important links and updated content. Twitter can be a fascinating tool just for reading. You do not need any special permission to read posts on Twitter, as the majority of Twitter users enable their content to be publicly read. There are many ways to find content to read on Twitter, from searching for a particular topic and reading what the "Twitterverse" is saying about it to clicking on a specific user and reading all of his or her tweets.

Tip One of my favorite features of my Amazon Kindle is the "share to Twitter" feature, which allows me to highlight a key portion of the text in a book I am reading on my Kindle and automatically post it to my Twitter feed. Anyone following me on Twitter can see what I'm reading at the time, along with my comments, and they can click on a link to that book's product page on Amazon.

Posting Tweets

Posting to Twitter is as simple as typing a short sentence. You do not need to follow or read anyone else's tweets to post. You can post your updated content directly onto Twitter from anywhere you are using the Twitter website or the Twitter application on a mobile device or computer. Content you post on Twitter might be an activity you are engaging in, a thought you have, or a link that you like and think others will want to click.

LEARNING THE TWITTER LINGO

The 140-character limit on messages has caused Twitter users to create and modify their own shorthand codes to help users better use the service and communicate with each other. To help get you up to speed, here are a few of the most common "twitterisms."

Using Twitter, Eric Sheninger, principal of New Milford High School in New Jersey, formed a partnership with a company that donated technology equipment and training to the school. He states, "I used to be the administrator that blocked every social-media site, and now I'm the biggest champion."

"Social Networking Goes to School," posted June 14, 2010, www.edweek.org/dd/articles/2010/06/16/03networking.h03.html.

@Usernames

When a username is preceded by the @ symbol on a Twitter post, it becomes a link to that Twitter user's profile. When writing a post, you can publicly send a message to a user by typing his or her @username before your message. This notifies that person that you're posting about him or her. For example, adding @brianjdixon on a post that's asking a question about this book will allow me to directly receive a notification that somebody mentioned my book. Using this @username mention code is more powerful than just sending me a direct message to my e-mail address because other people can see what was posted and respond to or add to that message. This feature moves a conversation from a one-on-one exchange to a public interchange with many participants.

The @username shortcut also allows you to post information about other people. For example, you could begin, "I'm reading a book by @brianjdixon, and it made me think about . . ." This will allow other people to know about my book or to know about the content that you're reading, and users can directly click on the @brianjdixon link to see my Twitter feed. This automatic inclusion of a hyperlink inside of the message makes tweets much more social.

The mobile version of Twitter has a special tab for @username mentions, allowing you to view all of the tweets in which someone has mentioned you. At a live event, I search for the guest speaker's Twitter account and include his or her @username in my posts about the event. In this way I am instantly connected to everyone else in the audience who is tweeting about the same topic. They might write down a point that I missed or ask a really good question to which I would like to respond. It is this feature that helps Twitter become a collaborative tool for engaging in short conversations with other users.

> *Third-grade teacher Gaetan Pappalardo of West Deptford, Massachusetts, enjoys engaging parents and students alike through his classroom's Twitter page, creating awareness about special moments that happen in the classroom. He states, "I've committed to Tweeting one classroom/school 'little moment' of loving connection between teacher and student a day for each day of the school year."*
>
> "Engaging Parents: An Elementary School Teacher's Field Guide," posted October 13, 2011, www.edutopia.org/blog/parent -involvement-student-engagement-gaetan -pappalardo.

#Keywords

Another shorthand code that Twitter users have developed is the # symbol, or hashtag. The # symbol is used to mark keywords or topics in a tweet. For example, I could post, "Sitting in @barnesandnoble #writing my chapter on #twitter." These hashtags also become links, allowing other users to click on the keywords to see who else is talking about the same topics (in this case, writing and Twitter). Using the # symbol whenever you update your status allows you to include the subject of your tweet.

Retweets

When a follower clicks the "retweet" button on Twitter, your message is automatically forwarded to his or her own followers. This is standard practice on Twitter and is denoted with an "RT" at the beginning of the new post. When your tweet is retweeted, other users on Twitter will see what you've posted and can click a link back to your user account. This is a simplified way to give credit to the original author of a tweet you repost.

TWITTER FEATURES

Twitter offers several unique features to help you access great content, spread awareness, and receive feedback. These features include following and being followed, direct messages, twitter search, and trending topics.

Following and Followers

You can follow prominent people on Twitter to build relationships. Because Twitter is still fairly new, many foundations, nonprofits, and celebrities are much more accessible on Twitter than through other means of communication. They have developed systems and structures for filtering e-mail. They have gatekeepers for telephone calls, and most paper mail they receive is screened and shredded. But they still directly handle their Twitter account. Start by following their Twitter account and look for an opportune time to reach out to them. If possible, make your first introduction a reply to a tweet they have posted.

Another way to use Twitter is to share information with your own followers. Twitter users who follow your account will receive your updates, which are posted on their main page on Twitter. Resources you share on Twitter, including news, updates, and links, will be seen by all of the users following you.

Direct Messages

Twitter also allows you to send private messages to users who follow you. This is essentially an e-mail program built into Twitter. If the Twitter users aren't following you, however, you won't be able to send them private messages. This helps make the direct message function more exclusive and helps increase the value of the direct messages you do receive, because you'll know that they came from a trusted source.

> *Chris Wejr, principal at Kent Elementary School in Agassiz, British Columbia, states, "Twitter has become my own personalized human search engine as I am able to plug in to people with experience who can answer my questions. Twitter actually SAVES me time."*
>
> "Connected Leadership: A Journey," posted October 28, 2011, www.connectedprincipals.com/archives/4833.

Twitter Search

One of the most powerful features of Twitter is the ability it affords you to search for specific people, keywords, subjects, and places. The website search.twitter.com offers several advanced features for searching for specific tweets and Twitter users. If you are interested in a particular topic, such as "school lunch," you just search for that phrase on Twitter to see what everybody is talking about concerning school lunches. This is a really comprehensive way to see what is going on in the world around you. You can search for the name of your school or your city. You can search for a particular author or a news event. You can search for the subject of your next lesson plan. Using this feature is much more social than just scanning the news from major media outlets, allowing you to get a true feel for the zeitgeist at the time.

> *Peter DeWitt, principal of Poestenkill Elementary School in upstate New York, explains that Twitter is one resource educators should add to their list. "They will find blogs, articles, and videos that they would never be able to find on their own. There is just too much out in cyberspace to be able to find these resources through regular search engines."*
>
> "Why Educators Should Join Twitter," posted November 12, 2011, http://blogs.edweek.org/edweek/finding_common_ground/2011/11/why_educators_should_join_twitter.html?qs=twitter.

Trending Topics

One of the most interesting parts of Twitter is the trending topics. These are the ten topics being mentioned the most on Twitter at any given time. Trending topics will range from news, sports, and entertainment items to the ridiculous. Often these trending topics are keyword conversation starters that inspire the Twitter community to discuss a common topic. Examples range from "Finally Friday," for which users tweet about how excited they are that it is Friday, to "I love my mom because . . ." for which Twitter users post tweets stating reasons they love their mom on Mother's Day. What makes trending topics so interesting is that they have a snowball effect. When people start to talk about a topic, other people are curious about that and join the conversation. Tweeting on a trending topic can be a great way to engage in the worldwide conversation happening on Twitter.

Latest News

Twitter allows you to quickly catch up on the latest news. As soon as someone knows about a breaking story, he or she can post that information on Twitter, and within a few seconds that content is shared across the Internet. That is the power of Twitter. Worldwide events, from elections to government overthrows, have been broadcast via Twitter, bypassing and outpacing the mainstream media. Not too long ago it was announced that the president of the United States would be interrupting live television for a special press conference. Twitter was abuzz with speculations, and in just a few minutes the news had been confirmed and shared on Twitter—almost thirty minutes before the president had a chance to make his announcement. From checking football scores and learning the results of a live game to researching more important topics, such as elections and natural disasters, you can use Twitter to learn the latest news and how people are reacting to it.

ONGOING SOCIAL ENGAGEMENT WITH TWITTER

Twitter can help to build ongoing social engagement online (see Figure 3.1). With short 140-character updates, you can easily increase awareness of school activities, receive direct feedback from members of your school community, encourage collaboration by asking questions and starting conversations, and help others advocate for your school.

Nick Rate, a technology coordinator in New Zealand, explains that at Willowbank School Twitter and Facebook are being used "to provide continuous ongoing communication with the school community. This provides a flexible and adaptive online space with many added benefits including: marketing of events and needs reaches the widest possible audience[, and] business sponsorship possibilities through online advertising."

"Social Media at Willowbank School," posted October 15, 2010, http://centre4.core-ed.net /modules/page/page.php?space_key=382 &module_key=84275&link_key=55945&group _key=0.

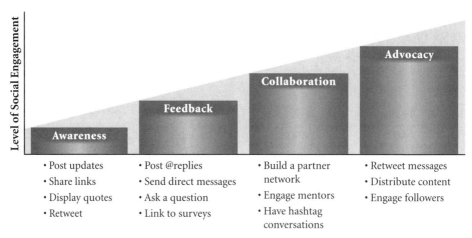

Figure 3.1 Social Engagement with Twitter

Awareness

Anything that you need your students or your families to know, such as upcoming holidays and important survey reminders, is a valid topic for Twitter. You can also use Twitter to post quotes and trivia that reflect your school's values and spread awareness of these values to your followers. You can even retweet news from other organizations, such as a summer tutoring program, to help generate awareness in your school community.

Feedback

You can receive feedback from your school community through Twitter. For example, you might send a direct message to someone on Twitter, ask that person a specific question, and get his or her feedback. You can also tweet out a question and get instant feedback from your followers. Or you could send out a link to an online survey that you've created using SurveyMonkey or Wufoo. Receiving authentic feedback allows you to continuously improve your communication and engage your target audience.

Collaboration

Twitter is the ideal tool for building collaboration. Because users are limited to only 140 characters, Twitter enables back-and-forth conversations with its call-and-response approach to posting online. Here are two tips for using Twitter effectively:

- **Respond to educational leaders on Twitter.** If you follow five or so educational leaders on Twitter, you will begin to see popular topics and upcoming educational trends. When a topic piques your interest, respond. You can do this by clicking the "retweet" button, which automatically includes a link back to that person. Notable leaders who would once have been impossible to get a hold of are now as accessible as a simple tweet mentioning their username. They will see that mention on their Twitter account, so if you are asking a question of them, they are likely to respond. This will help to begin an ongoing conversation.

- **Build partner networks.** Twitter can help you build relationships with other schools and nonprofits to share ideas and resources. Through frequent posting and responding to topics of mutual interest, you can build a network of partners serving a similar population or mission. When you need to brainstorm solutions to a challenge you are facing, use Twitter to reach out to this partner network.

- **Invite a conversation.** Another way to collaborate on Twitter is to reach out to another Twitter user by beginning a conversation. Good conversations often begin with a compliment and a question. A 140-character message is just long enough to include both. A sample Twitter outreach update might look like this: "@brianjdixon Love the new book, wondering about your thoughts on Google+." This is likely to get a response because it is short, it is direct, and it includes a compliment.

Advocacy

The sharing features of Twitter are what enable it to be such a powerful platform for advocating for your school. Using the donation website DonorsChoose.org, your followers can promote a link that allows users to donate to a classroom project. This information can be distributed through social networks further and faster than you could manage on your own. Simply by retweeting, Twitter users can share the link to this donation website with all of their followers—and their followers can retweet the content to their followers.

Hosting an event? Using a hashtag will help other Twitter users spread your message. Start tweeting early with a hashtag representing the event. Those interested in your event can search for your topic. Our school hosts a Project-Based Learning Summit with the hashtag #pblsummit. We tweet out this tag often before and during the conference. This helps keep the conversation organized, and it links all participants together. Anytime someone tweets about the event using the hashtag #pblsummit, we can see what has been said.

COMMON SCHOOL TASKS BEFORE AND AFTER TWITTER

Twitter can change the way you complete common school tasks, including directly reaching out to a local celebrity, reminding students and families about a school event, and finding great articles to read.

Task or Goal	Traditional Method	Using Twitter
Directly reaching out to a local celebrity	You would call the celebrity's office, write him or her a letter, or work your network to try to get his or her attention.	You can use the celebrity's @username tag to make direct contact with him or her on Twitter.
Reminding students and families about a school event	You would send a newsletter home, make phone calls, or post the event to your school website.	You can post the reminder on your Twitter account.
Finding great articles to read on your topic of interest	You would scan the table of contents of education magazines or websites.	You can use keywords on search.twitter.com to discover articles recommended by people you trust.

BEST PRACTICES FOR USING TWITTER

As Twitter continues to be adopted by educational leaders, more uses for this service will be discovered. Two best practices on Twitter that currently have an impact on school leaders are engaging mentors and professional development.

Engaging Mentors

Twitter is a great tool for directly engaging potential mentors. All Twitter users want to grow their followers on Twitter. They care about how many people read their posts, how many people are retweeting their content, and how many people are writing them back. That's half of why they post in the first place—to engage with their audience. So, become engaged.

Here's how to engage your educational guru of choice. Follow her on Twitter; when she posts something, retweet it, ask her questions directly, and comment on her posts. Over time, she will notice that there is a school that constantly retweets and comments on her posts. This can quickly help you begin a conversation with someone who a few years ago would have been impossible to engage. That's the amazing power of Twitter.

140-Character Professional Development

Twitter can be a great tool for discovering great articles and resources for professional development. There are two ways to find professional development resources on Twitter:

- **Search keywords.** If you are looking to learn more about YouTube as a tool for learning, for example, visit search.twitter.com and type in "YouTube in the classroom." A search on Twitter is preferable to a search on Google. Twitter content is curated, so all links are recommended by other users. You can even see who shared a given link and what other content that person has shared.

- **Follow experts.** A second way to discover great professional development resources on Twitter is to follow experts in your field who write or speak on your topic. Following these notable leaders will expose you to upcoming trends and valuable resources that they share.

GETTING STARTED WITH TWITTER

Question for Reflection: Write a list of local celebrities whom you'd like to have visit your school. How will you use Twitter to reach out to them?

First Steps

1. Have a few of your teachers conduct a Twitter activity in which they post a question related to their class content on Twitter once every day. Offer a prize to the best response from a student.

2. Consider how your teachers might use Twitter to engage mentors and speakers.

3. Ask for the Twitter usernames of your parents and community members so that you can follow them on Twitter.

School Website

Creating a school website that engages your audience is about more than just posting information related to your school. You need to use your website to continuously participate in a conversation with your school community. This chapter outlines the key features of a modern school website that help build ongoing social engagement across your school. It also introduces a twelve-item list of essential features of a school website to assist you in crafting your own. Chapter highlights include the following:

- Your school website is more important than ever
- Content management systems for today's websites
- Ongoing social engagement with a school website
- Common school tasks before and after designing an effective school website
- What to include on your school website
- What to avoid on your school website

- Advanced features of your school website
- Getting started with your school website

YOUR SCHOOL WEBSITE IS MORE IMPORTANT THAN EVER

Your website is the primary place your families visit for information about your school. When people search for your school online, they will wind up at your website. Consider how your website can serve as an information center for your parents by establishing procedures and policies that facilitate the posting of all important information and announcements on your school website. Social media is about building relationships online, and there is no better place to start than the school website, your main online location.

This chapter focuses on specific strategies and tactics to help you take advantage of the latest tools for engaging your school community through your school website. Covering topics ranging from collecting information and inviting engagement to establishing a content management system, this and the next section will assist you in either planning out or redesigning your website to better serve your school community.

Collect Information

Websites are increasingly becoming places to collect information from your visitors. You can passively collect visitor information by using Web analytics, and you can actively collect information using online forms and surveys.

A content management system, such as WordPress, has a built-in dashboard, or administrative panel, that automatically tracks data on your website visitors (see Figure 4.1 for an example).

WordPress is just one of several free website tools that allow for advanced Web design and management with very little technical knowledge. Through the dashboard, you are able to access website visitor statistics, including

- The total number of overall website views
- The total number of unique visitors to your website
- Which pages are the most popular
- Which links were clicked the most

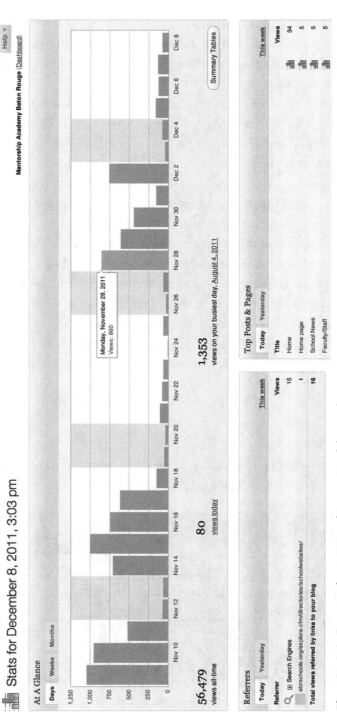

Figure 4.1 Screenshot: WordPress Dashboard

All of these data help you design a website that better meets the needs of your audience. The goal is to take information that is frequently accessed and put it in a more obvious place to make sure that your community is able to find and use that information easily.

Another method of collecting information from website visitors is to use online surveys. A survey does not need to be a comprehensive website evaluation; it could be as short as a question or two. Most online survey tools allow you to embed forms directly into your website using an HTML code. Embedding an online form takes care of all of the complicated design and website coding details, ensuring your survey questions and online form appear the way you want them to on your website. You could even use an embedded form as a teaser for a longer survey. For example, you might post a short question, such as "Which aspect of our school needs the most improvement? (A) bus transportation, (B) food service, (C) uniform policy, (D) parent communication" (see Figure 4.2). After selecting whichever response they agree with, visitors are directed to an invitation to take a longer survey stating, "Thank you for your feedback. To help us continue to improve our school, please take the following ten-question survey. It will only take a few minutes of your time." A user who answers the "teaser question" on the website is more likely to answer a longer survey once he or she sees how quick and easy it is.

Invite Engagement

Don't just share information; begin a conversation with your school community. When you use technology effectively to build relationships, your community feels

Figure 4.2 Screenshot: Survey Embedded on a School Website

a sense of ownership, which leads them to advocate for your school. Our parents and students are our customers, and our job is to communicate with them, engage in conversations with them, and invite them to participate with us.

CONTENT MANAGEMENT SYSTEMS FOR TODAY'S WEBSITES

As information is constantly changing, it is important to be able to update your website quickly and easily. Content management systems, such as WordPress, are built to make managing your online content as straightforward as possible. These systems make it both easy and affordable to update your school website on a regular basis.

Content management systems offer many features to help you better manage your school website, including multiple users, static pages, updated posts, content categories, keyword tags, themes, and plug-ins.

Chris Wejr, principal at Kent Elementary School in Agassiz, British Columbia, states, "Instead of only handing out our newsletters in paper form, we now have them in blog form so parents can offer feedback and questions."

"Connected Leadership: A Journey," posted October 28, 2011, www.connectedprincipals .com/archives/4833.

Heather Mansfield, principal blogger at Nonprofit Tech 2.0, writes, "Today, the often frustrating and expensive model for website creation and management that ruled during the era of Web 1.0 is completely avoidable and unnecessary."

Heather Mansfield, *Social Media for Social Good* (New York: McGraw-Hill, 2011), 7.

Multiple Users

Managing your website using a content management system allows multiple users to write posts, manage pages, and update content. Users have individual accounts and can update their assigned section of the school website. Different users can have varying levels of access. For example, administrators are able to change major features of the website, such as by adding pages or altering the navigation structure, whereas minor users are only able to update content on an existing page or article.

Static Pages

The majority of websites in the past were built based on the idea of static pages that do not need to change in title or major content. But the expectation today is for content to be frequently updated, and even static pages need to stay current. However, there is still a need to have static pages on your website that change only rarely—not everything needs to be changed on a weekly basis.

Updated Posts

Posts represent a different way to look at website content. These are posted in descending order, with the newest content always at the top. They usually include the latest news about the school, stories about current students, and any announcements and updates. Posts typically have a shorter shelf life than pages. They are more like articles in a newspaper, whereas pages are similar to a poster on the wall or a manual of operating instructions.

Content Categories

A content management system allows you to arrange website content in various ways and help the viewer access that content comfortably. In addition to the basic navigation structure on the main page, where you have a list of titles of the different pages and posts with a drop-down menu, you can have sidebar navigation with major categories of the pages and posts. If someone is visiting your website for the first time and is looking for specific information, clicking on a category in the sidebar would allow that person to view only the pages and posts that fit in that specific category.

Keyword Tags

A content management system also lets you add keywords to content. This process is often referred to as tagging content, and the resulting keyword tags are another way to organize the content on your website. If you have ever used Facebook, you know that you can tag a photo with the name of the person appearing in it. Clicking on that tag allows you to see other pictures of that person. The same is true on your school website. You can tag an article or a photo with the names of the people appearing in that post, keywords relating to that post, or any other relevant information. You can even create a tag cloud, in which frequently used keywords appear in a text bubble, with the words that are tagged most often appearing larger and the words tagged least frequently appearing smaller (see Figure 4.3). These tags help search engines navigate and reference your website content for more accurate search results.

Themes

Another feature of content management systems is themes. Themes are design templates that change the layout and color scheme of your website. Themes are easy to download and install and can be changed with only a few clicks.

Plug-Ins

An advanced feature of content management systems is plug-ins. These are small programs that expand the capacity and capability of your school website. Plug-ins help you not only better organize the content on your website but also bring in tools and content from other websites. Plug-ins enable your website to collect information from visitors; they let you upload multimedia files to your posts; and they display content that's automatically pulled from other social media tools, such as Twitter.

ONGOING SOCIAL ENGAGEMENT WITH A SCHOOL WEBSITE

Your school website is the best place to start building social engagement online (see Figure 4.4). It can be used to raise awareness, to collect feedback, to encourage schoolwide or community collaboration, and to advocate for your school's interests and activities.

Steven Painter, technology coordinator in Birmingham, England, explains, "I've used Wordpress to set-up the Fairfax School website using a custom theme that I created. In my opinion, it's an excellent choice for a school [content management system], as others are too bloated and overkill for a school site!"

"Wordpress for School Website," accessed December 3, 2011, www.edugeek.net/forums /windows/56968-wordpress-school-website .html.

Figure 4.3 Screenshot: Tag Cloud Created with Wordle

Three Steps to a New Website

Moving to a content management system is not as complicated as some vendors have made it seem. In fact, we upgraded our school website to WordPress for less than $500 in only a few hours' time. Here is the process we used:

1. **Find another website as a model.** Visit wordpress.org/showcase to view some of the best websites available online today. Decide on a design that you like, and use that as a model for your own website. Often you can purchase the theme that website was built on for less than $50. The Web designer you eventually hire will be able to quickly determine which theme was used.

2. **Hire a designer to import the content.** The next step is to share the content and design with someone who can set up your website. Although this process is not complicated for the experienced Web designer, it is worth having someone else to help you in this process. We were able to find a Web designer online at Elance for less than $200.

3. **Switch to the new website.** Designing your new website in the back-ground while keeping your old site live is key to a seamless transition. Once you are happy with the new website, your IT department or technology coordinator will be able to change the domain name settings to link to the new site.

Awareness

A school website can help build ongoing social engagement through spreading awareness of key information about your school. Traditionally the sole purpose of a school website was to provide the community with school-related information, and this is still the number one reason your community visits your site. With this purpose in mind, build a school website that helps community members find the information they are looking for as quickly and as easily as possible.

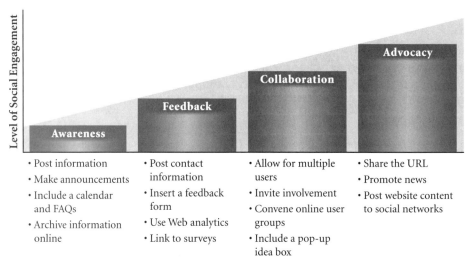

Figure 4.4 Social Engagement with a School Website

Feedback

Your school website can be a valuable place to receive feedback from your community. You can do this in a number of ways. First, by using a content management system, such as WordPress, and a social sharing plug-in, such as ShareThis, you are able to ensure that the community can give feedback anywhere on your website. Using the ShareThis plug-in, website visitors can click "like" on any article on your website. As the website administrator, you can view a list of the readers who clicked "like" and the comments they wrote on their social platforms using your ShareThis dashboard. WordPress even has a built-in commenting function that allows registered users to add their own comments at the bottom of every article.

> Florida educators Larry and Virginia Decker write that electronic communication formats (such as websites) give families access to homework information and require little time or effort to access.
>
> Larry Decker and Virginia Decker, *Home, School, and Community Partnerships* (Lanham, MD: Scarecrow Press, 2003).

Collaboration

Effective school websites invite collaboration. There is a tone to the design and the content that says to the Web visitor, "We appreciate your contribution." This tone can be set in a number of ways. When your faculty pages contain nice pictures of your teachers with their office hours and their e-mail addresses, you are inviting members of your community to engage, to reach out, and to communicate. When the contact information for your school is easily accessible on your homepage, you are inviting your whole community to engage. When the administrator's page includes a link to his or her personal blog or has his or her Twitter username and phone number, you are inviting your community to reach out directly to you with not only their feedback but also their own ideas. From initiating a discussion on a new topic through online user groups to brainstorming a solution to a common problem with multiple users, you and your school community can use the school website as a starting point for beginning collaborative conversations.

Advocacy

When parents hear from another parent that they should send their child to your school, they will visit your website. Does your website include features to allow your satisfied parents to promote your message Enabling sharing features is one way to build advocacy. When someone visits your website and shares the article on his or her Facebook page, that person is vouching for your content and essentially recommending it to his or her trusted network.

> By enabling school faculty to post forms and documents on their school website, Heather Carver, a district technology director in California, was able to help increase school-to-home communication and cut down on the use of natural resources. "Now, [students and parents] can download the day's lectures and homework assignments from the school's website."
>
> "Save Green by Going Green," posted April 17, 2008, www.edtechmagazine.com/k12 /article/2008/04/save-green-by-going-green.

COMMON SCHOOL TASKS BEFORE AND AFTER DESIGNING AN EFFECTIVE SCHOOL WEBSITE

An effective, engaging school website can change the way you complete common school tasks, such as distributing student handbooks, updating the PTA Web page, and undertaking a major website renovation.

Task or Goal	Traditional Method	Using Your School Website
Distributing student handbooks to get parents' signatures	You would physically print one paper copy of the student handbook for every student. These copies would be sent home individually with students on the first day of school or on report card night. Students would have their parents sign the back page of the student handbook and return the signature page to the classroom teacher.	You can post a PDF version of the student handbook on your school website for ready access by students and parents. A link underneath the PDF could be clicked to send an e-mail stating that the handbook has been read and received. The PDF could instruct parents to include their contact information in the e-mail. You would keep copies of these e-mails on file.
Updating the PTA Web page	Traditionally, PTAs would have their own separate Web page they had created outside of the school website. New PTA leadership often meant a new website because there was no unified system.	The PTA president can be given a unique login and the right to only manage the PTA page on the school website. He or she will be able to log in and make modifications to the content on the specific PTA page without the risk of changing other school Web pages.
Undertaking a major website renovation	Making a major change to a website, such as implementing a new design or color scheme, would involve hours of work and a large budget of thousands of dollars.	Changing the website is as simple as installing a new theme, which takes only a few clicks or a few minutes.

WHAT TO INCLUDE ON YOUR SCHOOL WEBSITE

When analyzing your school website, consider what types of information your families are looking for. The following twelve elements are a starting point for determining what you should include on your website to best communicate with your families:

- **Contact information.** The school's phone number, its address, and a link to driving directions should always be on your main page.

- **Faculty information.** To help smooth communication between parents and faculty members, include a picture, e-mail address, and classroom portal link for each teacher.

- **eNewsletter sign-up form.** Allow visitors to stay engaged by entering their e-mail address to automatically subscribe to your school's weekly eNewsletter.

- **Social media links.** Include links to all of your social media profiles, including Facebook, Twitter, and YouTube. This will enable your families to receive school information through their preferred channel.

- **Important links.** Consider the most frequently accessed resources that students and parents need, such as the online gradebook or PTA calendar, and include these links on your school website for easy access.

- **Recent news.** Feature frequently updated stories about students and teachers. Include interesting pictures and trivia to ensure that your website is a place that visitors frequently check.

- **Intuitive navigation.** The drop-down menu on your website should be audience focused, allowing both Web experts and beginners to easily navigate your site.

- **School overview.** Set the tone for your site to give visitors a better understanding of your school's philosophy by introducing your core principles on the main page.

- **Multimedia.** Including an embedded YouTube video or photo gallery on your homepage will help engage visitors, who are much more likely to interact with multimedia than to read static text.

- **Downloadable documents and forms.** Posting PDF versions of documents and forms, such as field trip permission slips and uniform pricing sheets, will help you save time and paper and will serve as an efficient backup for important information.

- **Frequently asked questions.** A list of answers to the most common questions you receive can serve as an excellent resource for parents and can save your office staff time. As new questions develop, update this section to best serve your school community.

- **School calendar.** Consider using an interactive calendar, such as Google Calendar, for recording upcoming events and important dates. You can embed this calendar on your school website, and any changes you make to the calendar will be automatically updated.

WHAT TO AVOID ON YOUR SCHOOL WEBSITE

This list of common website mistakes will help you know what to avoid when creating or updating your school website. Once you see the list, you may be surprised by how often these items appear on school websites. If you see them on your website, it may be a sign that it is time for an upgrade.

- **Animated GIFs.** These small cartoons with simple movements scream OUTDATED WEBSITE. Not only are they annoying to the modern Web visitor but also they are distracting and serve no purpose.

- **Comic Sans font.** School websites from ten years ago, especially elementary school websites, frequently used the Comic Sans font. This cartoon-like font may have been novel at the Internet's start, but it is now amateurish and outdated.

- **"Under construction."** Never post that your website is under construction. This is no longer acceptable. Visitors who see "under construction" are seeing the final product. They are visiting your website right now. Even a "postcard page," a simple page with a picture of the school and basic contact information, will suffice in the interim while your website is being constructed.

- **Missing teacher photos.** It is so important that you post teacher photos on your website. In this age of Facebook, everyone has a picture online. Teacher pictures posted on your school website are important for parents who need to recognize the teacher when they come to an open house or a report card night. Require your faculty and staff to have their picture taken on student picture day. Use these pictures for the school website. They'll be uniform and clear, and they will look professional when hosted on the same Web page.

- **Broken or missing links.** Put yourself in the shoes of your parents and community members. They are visiting your school website to find important information. Visiting a professionally designed website and then clicking a link that says "page not found" destroys your credibility and frustrates viewers. Click through your website to check for any broken links and fix them as soon as possible.

- **Abandoned pages.** This is the most common problem on school websites. Pages created with the intention to update the content at specific intervals can cause problems for school leaders down the road. It may have been a good idea to post the annual picture of the football team on the sports page on your website, but if you're missing pictures from the last two years, that's not going to look good. Review your website for any pages with this type of "serialized" content. Either delete the content or set a calendar reminder to update the content in the future.

- **Outdated essential information.** Essential information includes the school's address and phone number, the name of the principal, the school name, and the school district—anything that would be detrimental if someone had it wrong. Ensure that updating your website is included in the transition plan whenever a major piece of information has changed at your school. Make sure that the essential school information is always current.

ADVANCED FEATURES OF YOUR SCHOOL WEBSITE

Here are a few ideas to help push your school website to the next level.

- **Squeeze page.** A squeeze page is a lot simpler than a traditional website, without any drop-down menus or complex navigation. A squeeze page leads to the full website. It can serve as a great introduction to your school, and includes graphics, a video overview, and an e-mail sign-up box. A squeeze page is a type of landing page that encourages users to sign up before being able to access that full website. Effective squeeze pages "squeeze" the e-mail address out of visitors by enticing them with free bonus content. A landing page is a specific page to which new visitors are directed, usually as the result of clicking on an ad. This lets the website manager monitor the effectiveness of ads and help guide new users through a process of learning about the school. Users can "land" on a squeeze page, thus making it a landing page, or land on another page of the website, such as the parent page or admissions page.

- **User management.** An advanced feature you may want to consider implementing is user management. Most content management systems enable unique log-ins for registered users to provide a customized website experience. Once logged on, different users view only the content that is relevant to them. For example, a parent log-in might automatically direct parents to the online grades and PTA sections. A student log-in might automatically link to the classroom portal page and online class schedule.

- **Live help.** It is now possible to have a person ready to engage in a live chat on your website when a visitor has a question. You can stand out from the competition by using a live chat tool, such as LiveHelpNow, to notify your office staff that a website viewer has a question, or by outsourcing these functions to a service, such as LivePerson, to answer website visitors' questions in real time.

GETTING STARTED WITH YOUR SCHOOL WEBSITE

Question for Reflection: How might you better delegate the updating of your website to ensure that content is kept up-to-date on a regular basis?

First Steps

1. Review the list of what to avoid on your school website. Remove any of these items.

2. Conduct an online survey, asking for authentic feedback from your parents and students concerning their thoughts on your school website. Based on their feedback, it may be time for an upgrade.

Ning

In this chapter you will learn how using Ning as your school's online collaborative network allows for an increased level of ongoing social engagement. Because many school leaders are wary of using such publicly accessible social media tools as Facebook and Twitter with their students, opting to use an online collaborative network that the school can manage, such as Ning, might be the solution these school leaders have been looking for. This chapter discusses the many pertinent issues of implementing an online collaborative network to increase social engagement throughout the school community. Topics include the following:

- What is an online collaborative network?
- How does Ning work?

- Ning features

- Ongoing social engagement with Ning

- Common school tasks before and after Ning

- Fully engaging parents in online collaboration through Ning groups

- Managing inappropriate content on your network

- Best practices with Ning

- Getting started with Ning

WHAT IS AN ONLINE COLLABORATIVE NETWORK?

To have a strong community that collaborates in decision making, you need to have a platform that serves as a schoolwide collaborative network. An online collaborative network is essentially a personalized website that members of your school community log in to. One such tool schools are using is Ning, a customizable, Facebook-like online platform that allows you to create a truly collaborative learning community. Ning features blogs, discussion forums, video sharing, and collaborative groups. The school administration controls who can use it, which features are enabled, and what content to approve. Implemented throughout the school, from faculty meetings to student homework, from online discussions to parent meetings, Ning can be a very powerful tool for encouraging a collaborative community across traditional boundaries of student, staff, and administration. All users have their own profile page, are members of specific user groups, and can send messages to other users on the network.

> *Implementing an online collaborative network enables your school community to interact in more authentic ways. Tony Bingham, the president of the American Society of Training and Development, and Marcia Conner, a management consultant and writer for Wired magazine, explain that these types of "emerging technologies enable a new kind of knowledge-building ecosystem with people at its core." The focus shifts away from the technology itself toward the relationships between the students, faculty, and parents in your school community.*
>
> Tony Bingham and Marcia Conner, *The New Social Learning* (Alexandria, VA: ASTD Press/ Berrett-Koehler, 2010), xvii.

HOW DOES NING WORK?

Ning is a tool that allows anyone to create a personalized, private online collaborative network. It requires little technical skill to sign up for an account and create a network, which only invited members can access. A Ning network is customizable, allowing your school to create the ideal collaborative network that fits your needs and is tailored to your students. You can change

- The network's appearance, including the school logo, the school colors, and the theme of the network
- The tools made available, including discussion boards, blogs, multimedia sharing, and groups
- User accounts, including who can register, their level of access, and privacy settings

Ning provides your school with an online portal for schoolwide collaboration. Community features, such as blogs, discussion forums, and poll questions, help make this site a great tool for today's classrooms. Having students complete and post their assignments on Ning gives teachers the ability to review student work and check for participation while allowing other students to view the contributions of their fellow classmates. Exemplary work can be featured on the main page to encourage and inspire the school community.

Bernie Trilling and Charles Fadel, board members of the Partnership for 21st Century Skills, write, "With today's and tomorrow's digital tools, our net generation students will have unprecedented power to amplify their ability to think, learn, communicate, collaborate, and create. Along with all that power comes the need to learn the appropriate skills to handle massive amounts of information, media, and technology."

Bernie Trilling and Charles Fadel, *21st Century Skills: Learning for Life in Our Times* (San Francisco: Jossey-Bass, 2009), 64.

NING FEATURES

This platform also hosts many advanced features that students and parents have experienced on such social networks as Facebook and Google+. Students adapt well to Ning because they are already familiar with popular social networking sites. This section outlines the main features of Ning, including profiles, messages, blogs, forums, groups, multimedia sharing, and the main page.

Profiles

Students each have their own page on which they can post video clips they've created in class; scans and photographs of their work or of themselves; and (my favorite part) a daily reflective journal, otherwise known as a vlog (short for video log).

Messages

Ning allows members to communicate with each other in many different ways. The network features an internal e-mail system to allow members to send messages directly to each other. Users can also comment on each other's content and pages directly. Administrators can send message blasts to the entire network with only a few clicks.

Blogs

One of the great features for student expression is the blog section on Ning. Each student's profile has a Web journal in which students can write, edit, publish, and share their original writing. This is a great outlet for student expression. Ning even allows students to read each other's work. There are many ways to use this feature to inspire collaboration across the school community. For example, you might have the topic of the day posted on the main page of your Ning network for the entire school to respond to in writing. In homeroom class, students could be given ten minutes to respond to the question of the day on their blog. Then, during their English class later that day, they might be given a certain amount of time to read the blogs of other students and to write kind, specific, and helpful comments. This creates a collaborative community in which the students are sharing their voice and encouraging each other.

Forums

A discussion forum allows all of your students to give their feedback on a particular issue. Without such a forum, this type of interaction would be nearly impossible. Imagine hosting a schoolwide town hall meeting in which an issue is brought up and presented to the entire student body, and then every single student who wants to make a comment or ask a question is handed a microphone. Not everyone who wants to participate would be able or willing to do so. The

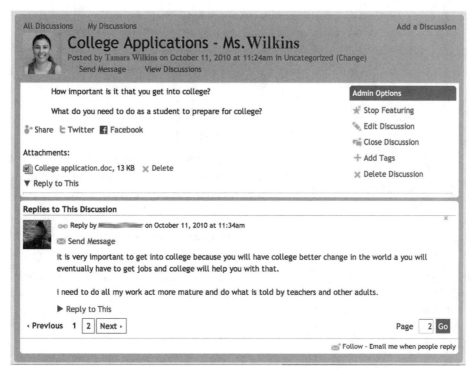

Figure 5.1 Screenshot: Class Discussion in Ning

technology of a discussion forum lowers the barrier to entry. Students have an opportunity to draft their response, check spelling and grammar, and make sure it's exactly what they want to say before they post it at their own convenience (see Figure 5.1 for an example of the class discussion feature of Ning).

Groups

From the student government association to the parent-teacher association, countless groups exist at every school. By using an online collaborative network such as Ning, you can manage all of the groups at your school in one location. Having them under one umbrella can save you time and increase collaboration. Also, remember that an online collaborative network that is managed by school administrators can be monitored, approved, and deleted if necessary. Requiring all student groups to use your school's online collaborative network enables you to ensure that the students at your school are safe. Your technology coordinator will be able to see who posted comments at what time, and he or she can set clear consequences for users who disobey the rules. This would be much more challenging using an unmanaged site, such as Facebook or Blogger.

Michelle Davis, a writer for Education Week, explored the use of social networking sites such as Ning to organize online conferences for educators to collaborate with other educators. She found that these social tools allow educators to collaborate on the latest trends and discuss pertinent issues in online forums.

"Social Media Feeds Freewheeling Professional Development," posted October 26, 2011, www.edweek.org/ew/articles/2011/10/26/09edtech-social.h31.html.

Multimedia Sharing

Many schoolwide collaborative networks allow users to post media files, including photos and videos. Students in an art class, for example, could take pictures of their unique artwork and post it to their profile on the schoolwide collaborative network. Other students can view the artwork at their leisure without time restrictions, and they can even post comments on the work and share the work with others.

Main Page

The main page on Ning allows you to feature key points of information for your entire school community to see. This could be student work, special announcements, a video, a discussion forum, a poster for an event, or any other important item.

Why Not Just Use Facebook?

Limited user management is the reason why Facebook is not ideal as a schoolwide collaborative network. With Ning, you can manage all aspects of user management, including creating a new user, assigning administrative rights, deleting old users, viewing user activity, and blocking or banning users.

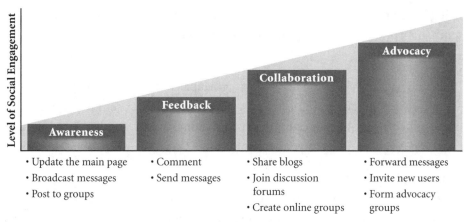

Figure 5.2 Social Engagement with Ning

ONGOING SOCIAL ENGAGEMENT WITH NING

As an online collaborative network, Ning is the ideal tool for building ongoing social engagement online, from encouraging awareness and feedback to fostering collaboration and advocacy (see Figure 5.2). This tool can completely change the level of engagement of your parents, students, and other school community members through multiple forms of interaction.

Awareness

Ning is a closed community, and so it is not necessarily a good tool for extending awareness to an external community. But it is a wonderful way to communicate internally to people who have identified themselves as members of the school community. Three ways to spread awareness across your school

According to Kathy Epps, information and communication technology coordinator at the International School of Central Switzerland, "The most interesting thing about the Ning format for me is the 'story,' or evidence of learning and growth, that accumulates as time goes on. . . . All students can read each other's thoughts and build on them. I find it interesting to see who dares to post first, and who tends to wait until the last minute to take advantage of the accumulated wisdom."

"Ning v Moodle," accessed December 3, 2011, www.classroom20.com/forum/topics/649749 :Topic:136867.

using Ning are posting updates on the main page, broadcasting messages to your entire network, and reaching out to specific groups.

Main Page
The main page of your Ning network is a great place to post information that you want your school community to know about. You could use this main page to share information about specific groups, upcoming events, fundraising efforts, or anything else happening at your school.

Broadcast Messages
One of the greatest advantages of using Ning is that you can easily broadcast a message to all of the members of your school's online collaborative network. This broadcast could be morning announcements or the weekly newsletter, but it could also be an important update that you want your entire school community to receive. This comes in the form of an e-mail, which is sent to the e-mail address with which the user signed up.

Group Conversations
Ning has many features that allow you to share specific information with a select group of users. For example, a teacher can post updated homework on her Ning profile page; this spreads awareness among her students concerning what the homework is for that particular night. Or the parent group can post an update making all the parents aware of an upcoming event.

Feedback
Ning has several features that make it a great tool for receiving feedback:

Messages
Using the message feature, which is similar to e-mail, you can send a broadcast message to all members of your network letting them know of an event or asking them questions. Then, anyone can respond directly to that message. That person's response shows up in the message section of your Ning account, and you also receive a copy in your e-mail inbox.

Forums
Forums are another dynamic tool for receiving feedback. Post a question on a forum, and other people can respond to it. The advantage of this is that others

can agree with responses that have already been posted and do not have to type their own response. These threaded discussions, which appear in chronological order, allow more people to engage in the conversation.

Commenting

The commenting and feedback system built into Ning is the ideal tool for encouraging student collaboration. Here is one example of how our school used Ning in our sophomore multimedia production class:

1. Students posted their final video projects on Ning.

2. Students from my other classes logged on to Ning, reviewed the videos, and left feedback according to very clear benchmarks and guidelines. These included the following:

   - No informal text messaging acronyms or shortcuts are allowed.

   - Comments must be at least three sentences long.

   - Responses must be specific, kind, and helpful.

   - The focus should be on providing constructive feedback for the content creator.

3. The original students read through this feedback and integrated suggestions into an updated version of their video, which was then reposted.

4. Students wrote a short reflection on the experience.

If you follow these steps, Ning can become a truly authentic, collaborative community—a place for students to present their work, receive constructive feedback and encouragement, and learn important life skills during the whole process.

Collaboration

Ning places collaboration as its foundational principle. This is the main reason why you should consider using Ning as your primary method of managing collaboration at your school. All other methods of communication have limitations, but an online collaborative network allows you to have ongoing conversations at multiple levels across time and space. Ning is like Facebook for your school, allowing your approved users to post their specific feedback and comments for a targeted group to see.

Advocacy

Although Ning works best as a private network for your school community, there are a few ways to enable advocacy within the network. Parents engaged in discussion on Ning can invite parents who are not engaged to join the conversation; and students can form advocacy groups to organize and mobilize support for specific causes.

COMMON SCHOOL TASKS BEFORE AND AFTER NING

Ning can change how you complete common school tasks, such as conducting Internet safety training, receiving and providing feedback on student work, and soliciting parent feedback.

Task or Goal	Traditional Method	Using Ning
Conducting Internet safety training	Students would attend an in-person assembly at which a guest speaker explained the dangers and risks that students face online. There might be a follow-up assignment or discussion in class.	In addition to participating in a training session on Internet safety, on an online collaborative network students have the opportunity to practice Internet safety principles in a structured environment with clear consequences.
Receiving and providing feedback on student work	Students would share their work in front of the class or participate in a gallery walk in which projects were displayed on a table. Other students would leave their feedback on Post-it notes.	Students can post their work on Ning at their convenience. Other students view each project and write comments below. This method allows more students to participate.
Soliciting parent feedback	You would distribute a newsletter that asked parents to send in their ideas, generating few responses. Only the most vocal parents would be able to share their ideas.	You can use a parent group on Ning to share ideas that you are considering and to ask for parents' specific feedback. Parents can respond at their convenience and will receive notifications of new responses.

FULLY ENGAGING PARENTS IN ONLINE COLLABORATION THROUGH NING GROUPS

School leaders are continually seeking out ways to increase parental involvement. Parents want to be engaged in their children's education and are always looking for ways to give back, yet many are busy and lack the tools and training required.

One way to increase parental involvement is to create a parent group on Ning. A parent group allows parents to ask questions, collaborate with other parents, and engage in an ongoing conversation about the overall school community. A parent group is also a great place to post announcements and upcoming events of which parents should be aware. You can even make one of the parents the group moderator. By providing this opportunity for conversation, you are opening the door to parents' becoming more involved in their child's education. Online social networks are becoming familiar territory for even the most technophobic parents. By hosting a parent group on your Ning network, you'll begin to see more parents posting comments, offering suggestions, and helping to coordinate events within your school community.

MANAGING INAPPROPRIATE CONTENT ON YOUR NETWORK

Allowing students to post content online means that you will inevitably need to deal with inappropriate content. School administrators and parents often wonder what happens when a student posts an inappropriate comment or picture on the school's online collaborative network. There are essentially two ways to manage this inappropriate content. The first is to block the content from ever appearing on the site. The second is to use content flagging to remove the content once it has been reported by the community.

Blocking

You can set up your Ning network to require that all content be approved by an administrator before it becomes available online. The technology coordinator (or members of the technology team) would simply view the content, make his or her best judgment according to a set list of criteria, and click "approve" or "reject." Content that is approved for posting is instantly available to members of your schoolwide collaborative network. Content that is rejected can result in a disciplinary conversation or consequences for the offending student. This strategy is a safe approach for training students to effectively use an online collaborative network provided by the school.

Flagging

With this approach, students are able to post content freely, following specific guidelines that are clearly laid out on the site. Once the content is posted, other viewers have the tools to respond, including a feature that allows them to click "flag" or "mark as inappropriate." When a post is marked as inappropriate a certain number of times, that content is automatically removed, thus empowering the community to police itself. This model can be quite effective for students in the upper grades. With the right user policy and agreement and the right training and consequences for students, this approach is the one that best serves students in the long run because it allows them to learn from their mistakes.

The Children's Internet Protection Act (CIPA) is a federal law intended to address concerns about access to offensive content over the Internet on school and library computers. CIPA requires that schools have an Internet safety policy that includes filtered Internet access; protections when students are talking through e-mail, chat rooms, and other forms of direct electronic communication; policies against hacking; prevention against unauthorized disclosure, use, and dissemination of personal information concerning minors; and measures restricting minors' access to materials harmful to them. For more information, visit http://transition.fcc.gov/cgb /consumerfacts/cipa.pdf.

BEST PRACTICES WITH NING

Implementing a schoolwide collaborative network may seem like a daunting task. The following best practices will help you experience a greater level of success. These tips include beta testing, user management, and password protection.

Beta Testing

Technology companies typically release a preview version of a software program before a final commercial release is available. This beta version allows advanced users to try out the software and give early feedback in an effort to improve the product before a massive public launch. A schoolwide collaborative network should be approached in the same way. Start beta testing with a small group of students or teachers and with a specific purpose, such as starting a book study group or a planning committee for homecoming. The lessons learned during this beta testing phase will help you design policies and procedures to use an online collaborative network across your school with a greater level of success.

User Management

The most powerful feature of a schoolwide collaborative network is the ability to manage users. Many of the problems occurring on social networks are a result of poor user management, whereby platforms take a hands-off approach to approving or removing content. By using Ning, your school has an opportunity to train students to use social networks in a professional manner. Here are three suggested steps for effective user management:

1. **Start with why.** Help students and parents understand the purpose of the schoolwide collaborative network. Host a training session at your school or online to make sure they understand the features and benefits.

2. **Establish a user agreement.** Implement clear expectations and consequences with a user agreement. Make signing this agreement a requirement before receiving a Ning account.

3. **Delegate.** Share the responsibilities of user management by developing clear processes for approving content, banning users, and deleting accounts.

Password Protection

One lesson for students to learn is the importance of account management. In today's digital age, students will have ten to twenty different usernames and passwords for their multiple online profiles. As they get older and more independent, students will establish a number of these profiles on platforms ripe for security risks, from online banking and bill pay to membership networks at home, school, and work. Account management, including remembering multiple usernames and passwords, is now an important life skill for all students.

It is important for students to use a strong password whenever they create a username and profile. This simple life lesson can prevent identity theft that leaves negative marks on their credit rating, their bank account history, and their online identity.

Practices that lead to a strong password include using both letters and numbers; using 1337speak (elite computer speak), whereby numbers represent letters and letters represent numbers; using capitalization strategically; and adding an element of the nonsensical. A password that I have used in the past was "Panda57!" Even if someone were to follow me around all day long and study my life, they would never be able to guess this password. It includes a capital letter, numbers, and an exclamation point. Over time, I increased the strength of my password, changing the first "a" to "@" and adding a different lowercase letter in front of the password for each site. For example, my eBay password at the time was "eP@nda57!" My Facebook password was "fP@nda57!" The chance of someone figuring out this pattern is very low. And don't worry, I use a different password now.

GETTING STARTED WITH NING

Questions for Reflection: What networks are you currently a member of? What value have you seen from your participation? How might your school's parents respond to a parent group on Ning?

First Steps

1. Create a Ning group to allow your teachers to discuss a book they are reading. Ask them to create their own profile and use Ning to blog on their reaction to the book.

2. Invite five colleagues to join a Ning group you create. The group Baton Rouge High School Principals would feature school leaders from the area discussing pertinent issues and collaboratively solving problems.

3. Challenge one teacher to create a Ning group for his or her class. Join this group and contribute to the discussion. Use the lessons learned to encourage the rest of the faculty to join the online collaborative network.

YouTube

YouTube is the world's most popular video sharing site, and it can also be a school's most powerful social media platform. This chapter provides school leaders with several effective methods for using YouTube to increase social engagement, and includes the following topics:

- How YouTube works
- Interacting with YouTube
- Ongoing social engagement with YouTube
- Classroom teaching with YouTube
- Other ways to use YouTube
- Getting started with YouTube

Your school can greatly benefit from using YouTube. It allows you to search for and watch videos on almost any topic, and it also lets you post your content to this major platform that anyone can access. YouTube is truly TV for you, taking the power of television to tell stories and share content and placing it into the hands of every visitor. The "You" in YouTube is what makes it such a powerful platform. If a picture is worth a thousand words, then video must be worth a million.

YouTube is now one of the first places people go to get new information. YouTube links even show up as top search results on Google. As video is an engaging medium, searchers may be more likely to click on video search results over traditional websites.

HOW YOUTUBE WORKS

To truly understand the power of YouTube, it is important to see the basic way in which a video is shared:

1. **A video is created.** The first step is making a video. This may be a webcam video created in response to a question, a video of a conference presentation, or a highly produced music video with multiple camera angles, titles, and sound. Except for adult content, no topic or format is off-limits on YouTube.

2. **The video is uploaded to YouTube.** Next, the user logs in to his or her account and uploads the video. The user has the option to include keyword tags and a description of the video. These "metadata" help the video appear in the search results for those keywords. The description also offers context, allowing the user to write an explanation of the video and include links to further resources.

3. **The video is converted and posted to the site.** Usually the video is converted and processed in only a few minutes. YouTube allows users to upload nearly any format of video and then convert it into a friendlier format (Flash or HTML5) after the video is uploaded to ensure that anyone on any device with any connection speed can view it.

4. **Networks are notified.** Once the video is online, the sharing begins. All of the user's subscribers receive a notification of the new video. The video is automatically shared with other social networks, including Facebook and

Twitter. Finally, the search database is updated, ensuring that people who search for that topic or keyword will find the video.

5. **Viewers interact with and respond to the video.** As a social media platform, YouTube features several tools for audience engagement. These tools include

- *Video rating system.* YouTube allows viewers to "like" or "dislike" content. Good content gets "liked." These likes help good videos rise to the top of search results on YouTube, increasing their exposure to a larger audience of viewers.

- *Comments.* Viewers post text comments and links that appear below the video.

- *Responses.* Viewers are able to post video responses, adding additional content, providing context to the video, or rebutting what is being said in the video. This helps to create a conversation.

- *Sharing through Facebook and Twitter, embedding, and forwarding.* YouTube provides many tools for distributing content to other social networks beyond its own site. These tools help video content spread.

- *Tracked views.* As views are tracked, popular content snowballs to reach more viewers. Videos with the most views appear on the main page of YouTube, gaining more exposure to additional viewers.

6. **The video creator receives feedback and responds.** After posting his or her video, the video creator can view the interactions other YouTube users have had with the video. This may inspire the video creator to respond in several ways:

- *Create a follow-up video.* After receiving feedback, often a video creator will post a video based on the feedback he or she received to help continue the conversation.

- *Change the video's description.* The keyword tags and content description can be changed at any time, allowing video creators to add links, disclaimers, and further descriptions.

- *Respond to comments.* The video creator can post his or her own comments in response to the ones received, creating a two-way dialogue about the video in an interactive format.

INTERACTING WITH YOUTUBE

You do not need to be a video creator to effectively use YouTube to benefit your school. Here are six basic ways that users interact with YouTube, with examples from the educational world:

- **Watch.** The most powerful aspect of YouTube is the amazing variety of videos available. Because anyone can post video content to the site, the types of videos you can watch are unlimited. There is also a growing movement to archive videos online: from conference presentations to TV shows, YouTube is growing its content base every day. According to YouTube (youtube.com/t /press_statistics), one hour of video content is uploaded to YouTube every second. YouTube is the world's largest video library, accessible for free to anyone with an Internet connection.

- **Comment.** Once you've watched a video and found it particularly interesting, controversial, or inspiring, you get to comment on it. Just below the video box is a text box inviting you to leave a comment. Before YouTube, this was unheard of. You'd watch a movie on TV, and you couldn't immediately share your thoughts, unless it was by talking with someone who was in the room, or maybe by sending an e-mail or calling a friend to say, "I just watched this movie, and here's what I think." But with YouTube it's immediate, and you can even type a comment while the video is still playing. The best part about this commenting system is that the person who uploaded the video receives a notification that someone has commented on it.

- **Share.** Once you've found a video that you like or that's worth talking about, you can also share that video. Click the e-mail button, the Facebook button, or the Twitter button; as long as you're logged in to the social network of your choice, that video will instantly pop up on your profile for all of your friends to see. This will help that video be seen by more people. You can share the video on your school website, blog, or classroom portal by simply copying the video's URL and pasting it into your site.

- **Respond.** An innovative way to use YouTube is to post a video response on a popular or relevant topic. Video responses can begin a conversation and will receive much more attention from both the viewers and the person who uploaded the original video than would written comments. For example, if your local news station posts clips of its reports on YouTube, you as the school leader can post a video response to a news story, giving your own take on the issue at hand. Each of your videos could have a text-based link that refers viewers back to your school website.

- **Organize.** You can organize all of your uploaded videos in one place on your YouTube channel. This allows you to highlight specific videos for first-time viewers. Check out our school's YouTube channel at youtube.com /MentorshipAcademy. One great feature of your YouTube channel is the "favorites" section, which allows you to designate other videos on YouTube as your favorites, representing your school's philosophy, supporting your school's methodology, or just showing your school's personality.

- **Upload.** Creating videos is much easier than it used to be. Most computers have a built-in webcam. To create a video, simply open Windows Movie Maker or iMovie, click the camera icon, and begin recording. Once finished, just click "upload" and enter a description of the video. Most cell phones now have video cameras and Internet built in, allowing you to upload videos to YouTube on the go.

ONGOING SOCIAL ENGAGEMENT WITH YOUTUBE

YouTube is a dynamic tool for increasing your school's ongoing social engagement (see Figure 6.1). YouTube allows you to build awareness, receive feedback,

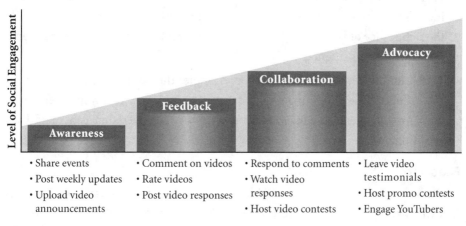

Figure 6.1 Social Engagement with YouTube

collaborate with your school community, and empower your followers to advocate for your school. Videos provide an authentic inside look at your school.

Awareness

Online videos that share happenings at your school are perfect for building awareness, allowing you to reach a larger audience with an authentic message. Start with weekly announcements on YouTube. By posting weekly video announcements, you can share information across your school community.

YouTube is a great place to feature interesting events at your school. Here are a few ideas of what to post:

- Clips from performing arts events.
- Videos from sporting events, such as a highlight reel of the football game.
- An interview with a star student in academics, performing arts, or sports.
- Videos featuring teachers, particularly if they're interviewed by a student.
- Facility updates, for example a video tour of a construction project with the principal showing off your new learning space.
- Faculty spotlights featuring various members of your school community, including cafeteria staff, paraprofessionals, and others who are not necessarily the public face of your school but who have a dramatic impact on your school's operations and students.
- Event announcements featuring, for example, the student council president talking about the upcoming spring dance. This type of video would help build buzz for the event and may even increase turnout over that generated by a traditional paper-based flyer or newsletter.

Feedback

YouTube is a great medium for providing feedback because you can ask a question in a video and get immediate responses. This can happen through the commenting feature, which as already mentioned allows viewers to post a text comment immediately underneath your video or to add a video response. You don't even need to ask a question. Post a video announcing the football game, and you'll get comments on your video from students, parents, alumni, and maybe even the opposing team.

Collaboration

YouTube can also be used as a tool for collaboration. A conversation can begin from one video response posted to a YouTube video. The original video creator views the response and creates a follow-up video to continue the conversation. This leads to a back-and-forth dialogue between YouTube users that is publicly viewable, encouraging other users to get involved in the conversation. You can also collaborate with other YouTube users on any topic you're passionate about by joining YouTube community groups dedicated to sharing videos and promoting discussion on specific issues. Or perhaps you have a contest in which students are to submit videos to propose themes for the annual dance, or ideas for the school mascot. Students from all across your school will post videos in response. Try this method to host online academic debates, prompting video answers to questions like, "What does the Second Amendment mean to you?" To encourage engagement, each student video response could be a raffle entry for a cool prize, like a gift certificate to a local restaurant or a ticket to the science museum.

"Use YouTube as a means to collaborate with other teachers," suggests New Hampshire technology writer Jennifer Hillner. Because YouTube boasts a selection of millions of videos, she recommends joining the YouTube Teachers Community (located at youtube.com/teachers) to find specific content that fits your needs and to post original student content for other teachers to discover.

"How to Use Online Video in the Classroom," posted August 31, 2009, www.edutopia.org /youtube-educational-videos-classroom.

Advocacy

YouTube is a dynamic tool for empowering your community to advocate for your school, for example by using video testimonials. Many nonprofits have used the strategy of holding a contest in which community members create videos advocating for them. Similarly, you could have your current students create a video listing the top three reasons why a student should pick your school to attend. This video could then be used on your website, shared online, and featured in a press release. Everybody loves a contest, and by empowering your audience to advocate for your school through community-created videos, you can capitalize on the buzz to help promote your event and school.

Another way to build advocacy for your school is to engage people who already use YouTube. You could reach out to other "YouTubers," content creators on YouTube who have developed a following, asking them to help promote an event or contest at your school. You might also partner with a local nonprofit in your community that regularly uses YouTube. Perhaps the nonprofit will add a short commercial, or introduction, for your school. YouTube now also allows for video advertising, so you can post a short five- to ten-second video promoting your school to play as an ad before videos. YouTube follows the same cost-per-click and cost-per-impression pricing structure that Facebook does with its ads. To learn more, revisit Chapter Two.

Have Some Fun Online

YouTube and other social media outlets allow you to have some fun online. At the end of the school year, a team of teachers and I got together and created a music video, rewriting the lyrics to a popular song. We played the video for students at the end of our school's talent show. The students enjoyed the video, and many wanted to watch the video again. That evening I posted the video on my YouTube account and was amazed to receive several hundred views overnight. The video spread like wildfire. The comments below the video were especially encouraging. This silly video for a talent show that I posted on YouTube brought much more attention to our school than a $3,000 radio campaign on the local radio station. YouTube is a powerful tool that everyone online uses, so consider creative ways to take advantage of it.

CLASSROOM TEACHING WITH YOUTUBE

This section outlines several ideas to help your teachers use YouTube in the classroom, such as finding creative ways to prerecord and use video lectures. Students also have fun creating videos, so YouTube can be used as a way get students excited about class projects.

Video Lectures

Many teachers are amazed to discover the power of being able to use video wherever they are. The reality is that kids have a higher expectation of how multimedia is used in the classroom now than they did in the past.

For example, a teacher might start each class with a YouTube video. This is a great way to get students' attention and to make a connection between classroom content and the real world. While planning the class for the next day, the teacher can record a short video at home, saying, "Guys, I'm really excited. Today, this is what we are going to learn . . ." As the students enter class the next day, a student helper can press "play" on the video, allowing the teacher to take attendance and handle other issues while students prepare for the lesson by watching the video.

Louisiana middle school math teacher Nancy Grunewald had her students create original videos teaching classroom content, which they posted on YouTube. She explains, "The students really came up with some clever ideas." One group's video has already been viewed over a thousand times. She also recommends that students create videos at the end of a unit. "This would allow for an informal assessment and/or a mini-review before a formal assessment."

"Engaging Students in the Classroom Using YouTube," accessed April 22, 2012, www .lamath.org/journal/vol5no1/Engaging _Students.pdf.

Classroom instructors who teach multiple sections of the same content are often concerned about maintaining their level of energy throughout the day. Instead of "faking it" for each class, the teacher could put in a little effort ahead of time and record the lesson. You might go and take a walk out in the snow or on the beach with notes and a camera in hand. Talk to the camera as if it were the classroom full of students. Deliver the lecture there, on camera, and try to keep it around ten minutes. Then play it for each class. By doing this, teachers gain forty to sixty minutes a day, depending on their teaching load. This additional time will allow them to walk around and check on students individually. The students will enjoy it because they get a glimpse into the teacher's life away from school. Of course, these videos can also be archived online and played back at home for students to review. If a teacher has to miss a day because he or she is sick, then the substitute teacher can still play the video for the class.

Flipped Classroom

Although it is generally true that schools block access to YouTube on their school network, students with Internet access at home will be able to view these online videos at their convenience. In a traditional classroom, the teacher teaches the students, and they take notes, study at night, and take a quiz the next day. The homework is given after the class. The flipped classroom puts homework first, focusing assignments on preparing students for the class. Online video tools such as YouTube can be used to flip the classroom by having students watch a video for homework that prepares them for a discussion in the class the following day. Watching a video at home feels a little less like homework and can help engage all students.

Darren Nelson, who teaches algebra in Winston-Salem, North Carolina, describes the benefits of creating video lectures for students to watch at home. "This saves an amazing amount of time. We can demonstrate a math concept in a 10-minute video that normally we'd spend a whole period on in class. Students work at their own pace and, if they finish the problems in class, they move on to the next lesson."

"Inside the Flipped Classroom" by Kathleen Fulton, accessed April 22, 12, http://thejournal .com/articles/2012/04/11/the-flipped-classroom .aspx.

Student-Created Projects

Students can create authentic videos in and outside of class to have an impact on the classroom community and on student learning. Student videos contribute to a high level of engagement because peers will want to watch other students' recorded projects. For example, a classroom teacher could divide the class into small groups and assign each group a foundational concept from the course. The group would research the concept and create a video teaching that concept. The classroom teacher could use this video anytime that content is covered in class. From amusing attention getters to straightforward reviews, videos in this growing library of student-created tutorials can help keep the classroom engaged. Asking students to create videos in a group can have a lasting impact on student learning and achievement.

Inspirational Videos

Given that YouTube is the world's largest online library of videos, it's not surprising that many of these videos can be used to inspire students. From historical footage to current news events, the videos on YouTube are as varied as you could imagine. Take, for example, a novel that students are studying in class. Simply searching on YouTube for the title of that novel could reveal many different types of videos. This includes video book reviews that readers of different ages have written and recorded. Watching these book reviews allows students to get a different perspective on the novel they are reading, other than just the teacher's or that of a fellow classmate. Other videos that may inspire your students include dramatic interpretations, TED videos, and video tutorials:

- **Dramatic interpretations.** Many of the novels that are typically studied in K–12 settings have been fodder for student projects for a number of years. When students create a video project for a particular novel, it is not uncommon for them to post this video on YouTube. Your students can benefit from watching these various novel interpretations and even creating their own.

- **TED videos.** One of my favorite websites is TED, which stands for technology, entertainment, and design. These short videos feature inspiring speeches from the world's greatest thinkers. TED videos are ideal for inspiring school community conversations. If you've never visited this site, you are missing out.

- **Video tutorials.** Teachers from across the country regularly post tutorials on YouTube. Sharing their best practices not only benefits their class but also inspires other students online. Imagine how your dynamic explanation of an algebraic concept could be used by teachers across the country to challenge their students.

Annotated Adventures

Use the annotations feature to link videos together, creating a "choose your own adventure"–type experience. The live annotations allow you to point to specific points in videos, creating an interactive storytelling experience. Annotations are the most dynamic YouTube feature for inspiring students because they serve as interactive Post-it notes. If, for example, the teacher creates a video asking a question that some students may need more background information to answer, the teacher can create an annotation at that moment in the video. A student who is confused or requires additional information can then simply click the annotation to visit a website that contains the needed information. Students who understand the content can simply continue watching the original video. This interactive feature moves YouTube from a passive medium to an interactive platform, enabling students to get information in real time.

YouTube Alternatives

One of the challenges preventing school administrators from allowing YouTube is not necessarily the videos themselves but rather all of the negative, explicit, or superfluous comments. Two sites give you the power of online YouTube videos without the unnecessary comments: SafeShare.TV and ViewPure. If YouTube is blocked, you can download YouTube videos to a computer hard drive or memory stick using KeepVid. To watch just a short clip of a long YouTube video, check out YouTube Time. Finally, it is worth mentioning that although it has merely a fraction of the content of YouTube, some educators love TeacherTube, which only displays video content approved by a staff of teachers.

OTHER WAYS TO USE YOUTUBE

Teachers and school administrators are continuing to discover and test new ways to use YouTube throughout the school community. YouTube has been an effective medium for communicating with the external community as well.

Recruiting Students with YouTube

Put yourself in the shoes of potential students. They want to know who their teachers would be. They want to know what kind of school they might attend. By finding your school on YouTube, these students are going to be impressed. They'll think your school is cool and current, and they'll be excited to know what other ways you integrate today's technology in the classroom.

Figure 6.2 Screenshot: Teacher Recruiting Video

Recruiting Teachers with YouTube

You can differentiate yourself and your school by using YouTube to recruit teachers. Here are the steps we followed at Mentorship Academy to recruit our incredible teaching team:

1. Create a video introducing your school, touring the facilities, and highlighting why potential teachers should work there (see Figure 6.2 for an example of what such a video might look like).

2. Post this video on YouTube, and embed it on your website and include a link in your craigslist job postings.

3. Ask applicants to create their own introductory videos to be sent in before they are interviewed. You'll be surprised by the results.

GETTING STARTED WITH YOUTUBE

Questions for Reflection: Does your school block YouTube for students? What policies and procedures would you have to put in place before unblocking YouTube? How could this work?

First Steps

1. Visit YouTube and search on a relevant topic, such as "classroom management" or "better meetings." Search results are typically sorted by keyword relevance. Try sorting the results by views, ratings, and upload date—these advanced filters can help you discover higher-quality content.

2. Using your computer's webcam, record and upload a video response to another YouTube video. You may want to start by responding to a review of a book you have read or a news story affecting your local area.

Online Surveys

Online survey tools allow you to quickly and easily gather authentic feedback from your school community. Topics covered in this chapter include the following:

- Surveys are now social
- Survey tools
- Ten steps to online survey success
- Features of online surveys
- Planning an online survey
- Ongoing social engagement with online surveys
- Common school tasks before and after online surveys
- Survey filtering and chart creation

- Online surveys in the classroom
- Getting started with online surveys

SURVEYS ARE NOW SOCIAL

Social media is about engaging your community in a conversation. A tried-and-true method of receiving feedback is the survey. Online survey tools integrate into your social media strategy to help make gathering authentic feedback from your school community easier than ever. Online surveys are essential to gathering authentic feedback from your school community—and receiving authentic feedback and compiling the data you receive will help you better incorporate social media in the school experience. Learn what you are doing well and discover ways that you can better serve the needs of your community by conducting regular surveys.

At Mentorship Academy we've used online surveys to collect and analyze feedback from several groups:

- **Students.** We've used surveys with students to evaluate the overall school experience and to improve our internal systems, including bus transportation and food service, as well as our uniform policy.

- **Parents.** Seeking to increase parental engagement in children's education, we've used surveys to learn about parents' technology use and attitudes to improve our communication strategy.

- **Teachers.** Surveys have helped secure anonymous feedback from our teachers about their job satisfaction to help prevent teacher burnout and eliminate unnecessary administrivia.

- **Community members.** A survey gauging community members' interest in mentoring students at our school was an effective tool to understand how we might better reach out to potential volunteers.

SURVEY TOOLS

There are several online survey tools to choose from, each with different features and benefits. The three tools we have used at our school are SurveyMonkey, Wufoo, and Checkbox Online. Each of these survey tools allows you to quickly construct surveys, distribute them to the appropriate audiences, and place them on your website or other social media platforms. SurveyMonkey seems to be the most popular survey tool in the education field because it is easy to use. Wufoo is the best tool for embedding survey questions on your website as an online form. Their exportable charts and graphs are the best around. An advanced tool we've begun to explore is Checkbox Online, which allows for survey branching and scoring. Branching is a feature that dynamically adjusts the questions a user sees based on his or her response to a previous question. Scoring allows you to assign point values to answers, offering a total score for survey takers at the end of the survey. All three of these tools offer a free trial, so take the time to discover the tool that is right for you.

TEN STEPS TO ONLINE SURVEY SUCCESS

To use online surveys effectively, follow this straightforward process:

1. **Select your audience.** Consider the audience you would like to survey. Whom are you going to be asking questions? Parents, students, teachers, community members?

2. **Define the outcomes.** What key information are you looking to receive? Are you looking for specific examples of a certain situation, or to get an overall impression of your prospective target audience? Clearly defined objectives will help you write better survey questions, help you know what to include in the survey invitation, and help you analyze the results.

3. **Construct the questions.** Knowing what you are looking for, what you are asking, and whom you are asking is the foundation for creating a survey. Start with a piece of paper and write out a list of the questions you want to ask and the types of responses you are looking for. Rather than using the computer, starting on a blank piece of paper can help you stay focused on the goals of your survey. Now that you know these factors, write the survey in a way that helps communicate with the audience the information you hope to receive. Online survey tools feature many different question types: multiple choice, true or false, fill the in the blank, short answer, and others. When I design a survey, I look for correlations. Is there a relationship between this answer and this other answer? What trends can I notice?

The overarching questions you should ask yourself are, How are these data actionable? How can I use what I have learned from the survey to better help my students, better serve the community, become a better leader, or improve our school's standing in the community? Write your questions in a strategic way so that you can gather this type of information.

4. **Upload your questions.** Log in to your survey platform, click "create new survey," write one or more new questions, and select the question type for each. When creating an online survey, I have found it best not to overanalyze the questions, but rather to post them as quickly as I can. Creating a survey with unlimited options and many question types can be overwhelming, and the process can take a whole day if you let it. Set a timer for creating the survey, take the questions you have already written, and organize them. If possible, have your school assistant create the survey for you. Someone who is less involved in actually writing the questions can help write a better survey because he or she isn't going to overthink it. The great thing about an online survey is that you can always edit it later.

5. **Request responses.** Once the survey has been created and saved, you simply publish it and receive a Web link. This link is what respondents will need to access the survey. Use this link in an e-mail, embed it on your website, or even send it home in a letter.

6. **Track users.** Match up the respondents with those invited, and resend the request to those who haven't responded. Some online survey tools automate this process for you.

7. **Evaluate responses.** Once you've received enough responses to draw conclusions, begin to analyze the data you've received. Look for patterns and trends.

8. **Share results.** If possible, post the results of the survey on your school website, and share a link to the results on your social media profiles. Some online survey tools make it easy to share summary data with survey respondents through e-mail as well.

9. **Implement feedback.** Online surveys are useless until you use what you've learned. Review the results with your team and designate action steps to take based on your findings.

10. **Follow up.** A month or two after the original survey, send out a follow-up survey evaluating your implementation of the action steps. Seek authentic feedback to improve your practice.

FEATURES OF ONLINE SURVEYS

The many features of online survey tools help make them a dynamic method to receive feedback from your school community. The following are features of most online survey tools:

- **Survey templates.** Customizable survey themes and templates feature sample questions and include prewritten introductory and closing pages to help you quickly design your survey.

- **Question types.** Online survey tools offer multiple types of questions, including multiple choice, rank order, true or false, matrix, Likert scale, and open-ended.

- **Multiple pages.** Design your survey over multiple pages to help adjust participants' perception and focus. Long, one-page surveys receive lower response rates than surveys that have been made to seem shorter by placing a few questions on each page.

- **Instant results.** Share summary results with respondents immediately on the last page of the survey.

- **Data analysis.** Online survey programs include tools for creating summary tables, charts, and graphs to help analyze the survey results.

- **Branching.** This dynamic feature offered by some online survey tools adds or eliminates questions based on how a respondent answers the previous question. For example, you might ask, "How do you prefer to be contacted? E-mail, phone, or post mail." If they answer "Phone," the next question would ask, "When are good times to call?" This question would not be asked if the participant had replied with "E-mail."

- **Scoring.** Some online survey tools allow you to provide respondents with a score based on their answers. You can assign a point value to all questions or to specific questions. For example, if you are doing a survey about how to be more involved at school, the score could designate "gold star parent" or "silver star parent," or parent engagement could be a grade of 75–100 percent, 25–74 percent, or 0–24 percent.

PLANNING AN ONLINE SURVEY

Online surveys can be a powerful means of receiving authentic feedback from your school community. There are a number of factors to consider when seeking to use them effectively:

- **Survey title.** A descriptive title can help you stay organized and can communicate the purpose of the survey.

- **Survey instructions.** Because members of your school community may not be familiar with online surveys, walk them through the basic steps.

- **Sample size.** Any good researcher knows how important a valid sample size is to ensure the integrity of data. If you have a thousand students at your school, a sample size of fifty might provide authentic feedback from a diverse group of parents. If you only receive comments from ten people, generalizing those responses could be misleading, as the rest of the population might not feel the same way. Consider what a reasonable sample size is for each individual survey you conduct.

Best Practices for Analyzing Survey Results

1. Be sure to have enough responses for a representative sample.

2. Provide a paper version of surveys for parents without Internet access.

3. Offer an "additional comments" box to allow respondents to share their perspective on important issues not addressed in the survey or to provide context for their answers.

ONGOING SOCIAL ENGAGEMENT WITH ONLINE SURVEYS

Online surveys can help build ongoing social engagement online (see Figure 7.1). They are great for raising awareness concerning issues that affect the school com-

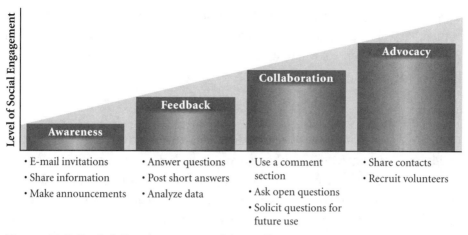

Figure 7.1 Social Engagement with Online Surveys

munity, are ideal for receiving feedback, can inspire collaboration, and can enable parents to advocate for your school.

Awareness

An innovative way to use an online survey is to communicate information and make announcements, letting parents know that certain opportunities exist by sharing them within the survey. For example, if parents were unaware that the PTA meeting was the first Thursday of every month, you could include this information in a parent survey and offer a chance for participants to win a gift certificate. Parents would then read through the survey for their chance to win the gift certificate, but they would actually be reading all of the announcements in a way that encourages understanding and builds awareness. Rather than just seeking feedback, surveys can be used as a means of making announcements to a captive audience.

Feedback

Of course, this is one of the strongest points of an online survey. Online surveys allow you to receive direct feedback from parents. Feedback on surveys can take the form of multiple choice, matrix, and true-or-false questions, but surveys should also be designed to allow respondents to answer open-ended questions.

This gives them a convenient space to share testimonials and provide their authentic feedback on specific key issues. Online surveys allow you to obtain direct feedback from your parent community with little effort beyond sending a link to your parent contact list.

Collaboration

Online surveys enable you to receive new ideas from participants. One way to build collaboration with an online survey is with a comment section. Asking parents for their comments, or allowing them to ask questions at the end of the survey, can help begin a conversation. By ensuring that you have at least one open-ended question at the end of every survey, you can hear specifics from parents on issues and topics that you may not have included or been aware of previously. For example, one question that I like to use at the end of every survey is, "Is there a specific question you wished we had asked on this survey?" We are likely to include that participant-generated question in a future survey, depending on the question's content.

Advocacy

Online surveys also help your parents advocate for your school, a process you can facilitate using the interactive features of online surveys. One way to enable parents to advocate for your school is by allowing them to share their contacts. In the course of the survey, if parents have responded in positive ways, invite them to advocate for your school. Ask a question gauging their interests: "Would you be interested in making phone calls on behalf of the school?" "Would you be interested in forwarding an e-mail to friends and neighbors announcing events at the school?" or "Would you be willing to share your contact list with the director of development at the school?" Parents could upload their contacts, pasting their friends' and neighbors' information in an online box, and this information could then be used by school officials to communicate with these contacts via e-mail. The e-mail would look something like this.

> Dear John,
>
> Zac Jiwa recommended that I reach out to you. I work with the Mentorship Academy, a project-based charter school located downtown. We are now recruiting mentors for our 2012 job shadowing day. Zac thought

you would be an excellent person to help us out. Would you consider volunteering two hours of your time?

If so, click <this link>.

If you are no longer interested in receiving communication from Mentorship Academy, click <this link>.

If we do not hear from you, we will follow up with a phone call in the next three days.

Sincerely,

Brian Dixon, Executive Director of Mentorship Academy

You can take this contact information and upload it to your eNewsletter's e-mail contact list, using a tool such as MailChimp or Constant Contact. By recruiting people through e-mail referrals, you are much more likely to receive a response.

COMMON SCHOOL TASKS BEFORE AND AFTER ONLINE SURVEYS

Online surveys can change the way you complete common school tasks, such as conducting parent surveys, inviting feedback, and recruiting volunteers.

Task or Goal	Traditional Method	Using Online Surveys
Conducting parent surveys	Surveys were printed, photocopied, and mailed to homes. Parents would fill out the survey and give it to their child to turn in at school.	A link is posted to the school website or e-mailed to all parents. As a reminder, a second e-mail could be sent to parents who didn't complete the survey.
Inviting feedback	This would happen in real time during a face-to-face meeting. The principal might stand up in front of the students or parents and say, "If anyone is interested in giving feedback on these issues, please see me after the assembly."	Schools can now maintain constant contact with the parent community. Surveys and feedback forms can be accessed online 24/7, and the data are easily archived online.

(continued)

Task or Goal	Traditional Method	Using Online Surveys
Recruiting volunteers	Parents and current school volunteers would be asked to pass out flyers to friends whom they thought might be interested. Chances are, many of the printed flyers would not be passed out. Volunteers could also be recruited by directly calling local community members.	With online surveys, potential volunteers can be asked a series of questions to better understand how they might be interested in helping. For example, maybe a local business owner is not willing to mentor students one-on-one, but she might allow a class to take a field trip to her facility.

SURVEY FILTERING AND CHART CREATION

You've sent out the link to your survey and have received responses. Now what do you do with all of that information? There are several ways to break down and process the data.

Exporting Survey Data

Online survey tools allow you to export all survey information, to be imported into a spreadsheet program, such as Excel. Both SurveyMonkey and Wufoo automatically create charts for exporting and explaining survey results. You are also able to upload the data you collect through surveys into an existing student information system to assist in updating phone numbers and other student contact information.

Once the data are in a spreadsheet, it is easy to categorize the information, focus on specific trends, and figure out how to respond. If one-third of parents are unhappy with the bus schedule, what actions can you take to show that you have listened to their concerns? If a majority of faculty members are feeling overwhelmed by technology in the classroom, what training can you provide to address their needs?

Tracking Feedback over Time

To help track data over time, you should conduct a given survey at least once a month using the same questions. This will allow you to see how you have improved and what you still need to work on. Leave at least one open-ended question to enable participants to regularly make suggestions, connect you to other members of the community, and vent their frustrations.

ONLINE SURVEYS IN THE CLASSROOM

Online survey tools are great to use with students because there are no right or wrong answers. Such tools actually show the number of students who chose a particular answer, opening the door for a discussion of how a student got the answer he or she did, or why one answer was better than another.

Instead of giving an assignment and saying that it is due at the beginning of class the next day, set a deadline, say by nine o'clock that night, to take an online survey. Maybe the survey is ten multiple choice questions, and students simply have to choose from among A, B, C, or D. The teacher can then see the graph showing the students' results, and can show that graph to the students the next day. This would cut down on a lot of the cheating that happens with homework, with students copying off each other on the bus or in the cafeteria before school starts in the morning.

GETTING STARTED WITH ONLINE SURVEYS

Questions for Reflection: Have you ever surveyed your students? What questions might you ask them?

First Steps

1. Ask teachers to give you questions they'd like to ask parents. You may be surprised at what they suggest.

2. Consider ways you can engage members of the business community through an online survey. A survey used to solicit their feedback can be a first step in building a relationship that could make an impact on your students.

E-Mail

An overlooked social media tool many school leaders could make better use of is e-mail. This chapter shares best practices for using e-mail, covering the following topics:

- Inbox overload
- A smarter e-mail system
- Advanced tips for using e-mail
- Schoolwide e-mail rules
- Ongoing social engagement with e-mail
- Common school tasks before and after e-mail
- Getting started with e-mail

Most school leaders struggle to manage e-mail. As a tool that is supposed to improve our efficiency, e-mail has only added more work and responsibility to our lives. Learning to use e-mail effectively is an essential function of today's school leaders. This chapter addresses the challenges school leaders face with e-mail and outlines a foolproof system for taming the e-mail dragon.

INBOX OVERLOAD

Almost every school leader is overwhelmed by the amount of e-mail he or she receives on a daily basis. When e-mail first came onto the scene, most people were excited. It was amazing to communicate quickly with anyone by just typing a few letters and an e-mail address. But over time e-mail has become frustrating, one more thing to manage, one more box to check, one more tool to learn. E-mail has taken over the majority of our work life. If you don't think that's true, try not checking e-mail from the time you get to school until lunchtime. Just give it four hours. You will be blown away by the magnetic pull that's attempting to drag you toward checking your e-mail. You won't know what to do with all of that time that's normally spent checking e-mail.

Because e-mail is something we have to deal with, we need specific ways to better manage and effectively use it. It's no longer acceptable to just ignore it. A former administrator of mine, when overwhelmed by the number of e-mails in his inbox, would just claim "e-mail bankruptcy," deleting all of his waiting messages. "If it's important, they'll get back to me," I recall him stating. Short of encouraging you to delete everything, this chapter outlines several key strategies for better using and staying on top of your e-mail inbox. For the sake of simplicity, the screenshots in this chapter focus on Gmail as the e-mail platform, but the concepts shared apply to other e-mail tools, such as Yahoo Mail and Microsoft Outlook.

A SMARTER E-MAIL SYSTEM

I have found the following tips to dramatically improve the handling of my e-mail inbox. Every e-mail that comes into the inbox is something to deal with. It is an unstated agreement made with the sender that requires action. When you open up your e-mail and realize that you have eighty-seven messages to check, and sporadically half of them have been read and half of them are still unread, it feels like you have a lot of work to do. A smarter system involves batch processing, four-step e-mail processing, setting up five folders, and receiving less e-mail. Use the following strategies to help you regain control of your e-mail inbox.

Batch Processing

The first rule in taming your inbox is batch processing. An e-mail is like a dirty sock. Action must be taken, and it needs to be washed. But do you do a load of laundry just for one dirty sock? Of course not. If you washed one article of clothing at a time, you would spend all day just doing laundry, much like many school leaders spend the majority of their day reading and responding to e-mails. Instead, by batch processing, you can check your e-mail less frequently, processing similar e-mails at one time. The key to batch processing is waiting until the "dirty laundry" piles up a little bit. More e-mails will be waiting in your inbox, allowing you to do more reading, deleting, and responding in one sitting. You will be more effective and more efficient in dealing with your e-mail by combining similar tasks and only dealing with them once.

Two keys to batch processing are keeping your e-mail program closed and checking less frequently. Keeping your e-mail program closed will stop the automatic notifications that alert you every time you receive an e-mail. Closing your e-mail program allows you to focus on important tasks rather than getting distracted every time you receive a message. Also, instead of constantly checking your e-mail, try scheduling specific times to check e-mail throughout the day. On most days I check my e-mail half an hour before school (in case of any last-minute changes to the schedule), then at lunch (if absolutely necessary), and again half an hour after school (to handle issues that arise that day). Each of these e-mail "sessions" takes about ten minutes, allowing me to keep an empty inbox and helping me focus on important tasks like writing this chapter.

Four-Step E-Mail Processing

Having a clear process to empty your e-mail inbox a few times a day can help you spend less time dealing with e-mail. Here are four steps to help you empty your inbox and respond to important messages in record time. Figure 8.1 shows you an example inbox before applying this formula. The process should be followed three times a day, and the whole thing takes less than ten minutes. However, it may take a lot longer the first time if you have let your e-mail build up.

Figure 8.1 Screenshot: Inbox

1. **Select all.** Start by selecting every single e-mail in your inbox (see Figure 8.2). You may need to change your view settings to display all messages. Selecting all messages will ensure that you deal with every single e-mail instead of selectively processing.

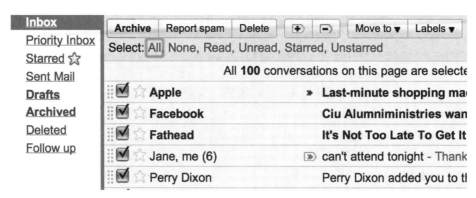

Figure 8.2 Screenshot: Select All

> **Tip** If you have thousands of e-mails that need to be processed, a quick tip is sorting by sender. This way you'll be able to quickly get rid of many e-mails from the same sender, such as eNewsletters or group messages.

2. **Star important.** Next, star each important e-mail you need to follow up on (see Figure 8.3). Scan through the list, clicking the star icon next to any e-mail you want to read. If your e-mail program doesn't have a star label, you can press the "control" key and click important messages to deselect them.

Figure 8.3 Screenshot: Star Important

3. **Archive the rest.** When you click "archive," all selected e-mails are moved to the archive folder. This removes them from the inbox but saves them in case you need to access them later. With the large inbox size that Gmail offers, there is never any reason to delete an e-mail. If you don't have an "archive" button, you can simply drag all of these e-mails into a folder labeled "archive."

4. **Review stars.** Click the folder containing starred messages to view all of the e-mails you need to read and respond to (see Figure 8.4). These are usually about 10 percent of the e-mails you receive. Process these e-mails following the "4D" formula outlined here, which shows four possible ways to handle a starred e-mail.

- *Do.* Respond right away. Write the e-mail response, unstar the e-mail, and click the "send and archive" button. This button is a time-saving Gmail Labs feature, further discussed later in this chapter.

- *Delete.* "Delete" the e-mail by archiving it without taking any action. Upon further review, you might realize that this e-mail does not require a response.

- *Delegate.* Forward the e-mail to someone else for that person to handle, and bcc yourself to include the e-mail in your "waiting for" folder (explained later this chapter).

- *Defer.* Add this e-mail to a to-do list on your mobile device to address at a later time. You might also consider forwarding the e-mail to a service such as FollowUpThen, which reminds you to respond to the e-mail at a later time.

Figure 8.4 Screenshot: Review Stars

Congratulations! As you can see in Figure 8.5, you have an empty inbox. This is something most school leaders never get to experience. Enjoy it while it lasts—until the next e-mail arrives.

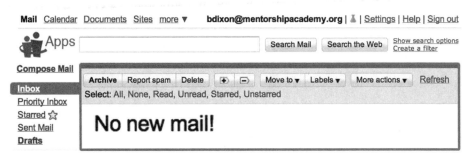

Figure 8.5 Screenshot: No New Mail

> **Tip** FollowUpThen is a service that allows you to defer responding to an important e-mail until you have time to do so. This takes the e-mail out of your inbox and sends you a reminder at a specific time you determine, usually a day or two later.

Setting Up Five Folders

With the virtually unlimited inbox size and advanced search capabilities some e-mail programs, such as Gmail, offer, all you need are five folders to manage your e-mail effectively:

- **Inbox.** This is where all e-mail is received. Processing your e-mail ensures this inbox folder is emptied three times a day.

- **Archive.** This is where all e-mail that doesn't require responding goes. Instead of deleting e-mails, move messages to which you've responded or that don't require any further action to your archive folder. There's no reason to ever delete an e-mail, unless there's an unusually large attachment. E-mails are just small text files. Archiving instead of deleting presents two advantages:

  - You may be able to use that e-mail somewhere down the line, such as when referencing someone's address that you do not have among your contacts.

  - Sometime in the future the issue discussed in an e-mail could become your responsibility. I have been in parent conferences in which an old e-mail was brought up, and I've been able to quickly access that old e-mail and use it in the meeting. Having an accurate record of parent communication does much to stave off potential conflict.

- **Stars/actions.** Clicking the "stars" label in Gmail or an "actions" folder in Microsoft Outlook will display all of the e-mails that you need to process following the 4D formula.

- **"Read someday" folder.** This is where you would put e-mails that you might want to look at one day when you have time. These may include eNewsletters, funny e-mail forwards, or listserve messages. Moving an e-mail to the "read someday" folder allows you to remove it from your inbox, but read and respond to it when you have time. If you have a moment when you really don't have anything you have to do, you can look through your "read someday" folder and see what's available for you there.

- **"Waiting for" folder.** This folder contains e-mails that you are waiting on a response to, which you will follow up on weekly. Once you've sent an e-mail that requires a response from someone else, bcc yourself and drag this e-mail into a "waiting for" folder. Check this folder weekly to ensure you've received responses to important issues. I usually check my "waiting for" folder on Friday afternoon at two o'clock. This simple tracking system has helped me hold team members accountable without nagging them. Implementing this approach to follow up schoolwide will dramatically improve the effectiveness of your entire faculty, helping eliminate important tasks being neglected or forgotten due to busyness.

Receiving Less E-Mail

Now that you have a clear system for processing your inbox, here are a few strategic suggestions to help you receive fewer unimportant e-mails.

- **Unsubscribe from eNewsletters.** Every eNewsletter has a link at the bottom of the message that allows you to unsubscribe. Click this link to stop receiving these messages.

- **Mark unwanted messages as spam.** Block specific senders by marking their messages as spam. This will set up a filter that will automatically move future messages from these senders into your spam folder.

- **Create filtering rules to bypass the inbox.** You can set up custom filters to have certain messages skip the inbox altogether. I automatically send most eNewsletters to my "read someday" folder, where I can read them later.

- **Change e-mail addresses.** If your e-mail address hasn't changed for a while, or if it has been displayed on your school website or been entered into an online sweepstakes or subscription service, you're likely to get a lot of spam. Consider asking your technology director for a new e-mail alias, and set up a system whereby messages received at your old address are automatically forwarded to a special folder in your new e-mail inbox. This will help eliminate unwanted messages.

ADVANCED TIPS FOR USING E-MAIL

If you are a Gmail or Google Apps user, Gmail Labs has features that add functionality to Gmail. Using just a few of these features can completely revolutionize the way you use your e-mail account. To enable a lab feature, simply click the "Labs" icon in your Gmail account settings, scroll through the list of features, and click "enable" on any interesting ones. My two favorite lab features are "undo send" and "canned responses."

Undo Send

This first lab feature can save you from some embarrassing situations. When you enable "undo send," a five-second delay begins between clicking the "send" button and the e-mail's actually being sent. If you realize you forgot something in the e-mail, you can click "undo send" to prevent the e-mail from leaving your outbox. How often have you been in the situation where you have forgotten an attachment, have forgotten to cc someone, or have forgotten to spell-check the e-mail? In those cases you have to send a follow-up e-mail asking the recipient to please ignore the first one and look at the second one. All of these hassles are eliminated with the "undo send" feature. When you send an e-mail a new text link pops up asking if you would like to stop the e-mail from going to the recipient. This appears for only a few seconds, with the default setting being only five seconds long. If you are happy with the e-mail sent, there is no need to do anything. If, however, you have forgotten to add a recipient to the e-mail or have forgotten an attachment, just click the "undo send" button. Sending is undone, and no one has received that e-mail. You are then returned to a draft of your e-mail to add the missing information, recipient, or attachment.

Canned Responses

A second feature of Gmail Labs that I highly recommend is "canned responses," which allows you to build a template e-mail with boilerplate text you can reuse. Today's school leader does not have to rewrite every e-mail that's sent to parents. To create a new canned response, first type out the full e-mail, including your subject line, and click "save new canned response." Name that canned response so you can use it in the future. When you find yourself needing to reuse it, just click "insert canned response" and choose from the drop-down list. I have found that using canned responses helps save me time. Here are situations in which canned responses work very well for school leaders:

- **Replying to job applicants.** Thank the applicant for his or her interest in the school. Give a short summary of the mission and vision of the school. Explain the job application process to the recipient. Finally, include an invitation for that person to follow up in a specified period of time.

- **Parent conference requests.** Start by thanking the parent for his or her support. Acknowledge the request for a conference, customizing the teacher name and the time. Then include the process for scheduling a parent confer-ence. Again thank the parent for scheduling and invite him or her to contact you in the future. For example, parents who e-mail me asking for the contact information of a teacher receive a canned response. I simply change the name of the teacher and his or her office hours to personalize the e-mail.

- **Internal human resources issues.** Canned responses can save you time when dealing with common issues and will help your e-mails look more professional because you've taken the time to craft that first template. Examples of these types of e-mails include an e-mail summarizing a teacher observation, an e-mail requesting a conference with a teacher, an e-mail asking a teacher to attend a seminar, and an e-mail reminding teachers to hand in their lesson plans.

Some of my other favorite Gmail Labs features to check out include

- "Send and archive." This feature adds a button that lets you send a reply message and archive the e-mail conversation in a single action.

- "Quote selected text." This feature allows you to quote the text you have selected when you reply to a message.

- "Auto-advance." After you archive a message, this feature automatically shows the next conversation instead of your inbox.

SCHOOLWIDE E-MAIL RULES

Establishing clear schoolwide expectations for e-mail usage can dramatically improve the efficiency and communication of your entire faculty. Three standard e-mail practices you may want to adopt and expect from your faculty include smart subjects, single-topic e-mails, and standardized signatures.

Smart Subjects

One way to communicate better through e-mail is to use the subject line to alert the reader as to your intention for sending that e-mail. Two e-mails I frequently send pertain to an article I would like the faculty to read and a meeting I want them to attend. For the e-mail with the article to read, I preface the subject with the words "READ ONLY: NY Times article." For the meeting, I write "RESPOND

PLEASE: Thursday meeting." Both of these "smart subjects" help clarify the purpose of the e-mail to help ensure the message isn't ignored or lost.

Single-Topic E-Mails

Another schoolwide rule to implement is to have one subject per e-mail. The key is to ensure that every e-mail is actionable, which means that the e-mail only requires one action. When one e-mail contains several items, it is more difficult to process. As an example, an administrator sends out an e-mail to the English department:

> **Subject:** Reminders
>
> **Message:** Team, let's move our Tuesday meeting to Wednesday at 3:30. I've attached an article for your review and discussion at the meeting. Also, please remember to announce to your last-period class today that money for the field trip is due by tomorrow. Students who don't hand in their money will not be able to attend Friday's field trip. Thanks, Janie.

The preceding e-mail should be divided into two separate e-mails. Using smart subjects, the two e-mails would look like this:

> **Subject 1:** READ ONLY: English department meeting change and article reading attached
>
> **Message 1:** Team, let's move our Tuesday meeting to Wednesday at 3:30. I've attached an article for your review and discussion at the meeting. Thanks, Janie.
>
> **Subject 2:** PLEASE ANNOUNCE to last period—field trip money due tomorrow
>
> **Message 2:** Teachers, please remember to announce to your last-period class today that money for the field trip is due by tomorrow. Students who don't hand in their money will not be able to attend Friday's field trip. Thanks, Janie.

Another approach is to replace the first e-mail with an updated calendar invitation. Google Calendar, for example, sends e-mail invitations and updates to all meeting participants. You can still include the attachment and notes about the article in the meeting invitation. The challenge we have experienced is that several members of our faculty had never used calendar invitations before, so a little training may be required to take advantage of this better system.

These two e-mails are more effective than one because the teachers can better process the separate messages. Both require action, so it's important for recipients to think of these e-mail messages as two separate, actionable requests. The first e-mail asks a teacher to update her calendar, probably printing the article attachment and creating a to-do item to read the article before Wednesday's meeting. The second e-mail requires a classroom teacher to remind students in her last-period class about field trip money. She may set an alarm reminder on her phone or write a note on the whiteboard for her last class to see.

The problem with including two subjects in one e-mail is that the most urgent item will be handled, but the most important one will be overlooked. In this case, students will be reminded that the field trip money is due (they've heard that before), but most of the English department will not read the article (unless separately reminded by a colleague, usually at the last minute).

When you write an e-mail that requires action, consider how you might help the recipient better process that e-mail. Make the e-mail actionable.

Standardized Signatures

Every e-mail that is sent out from a school-based e-mail account represents your school to the recipient. Keeping your signature and those of faculty and staff uniform helps your parent community better communicate with you and your team. The e-mail signature is an opportunity to help your school community access contact information, point them to important resources, remind them of the mission and vision of the school, and ensure professionalism. Here is an example e-mail signature you might want to include:

Dr. Brian J. Dixon

Executive Director

Mentorship Academy

339 Florida St.

Baton Rouge, LA 70801

Phone: 225–505–5013

E-mail: bdixon@MentorshipAcademy.org

Optional information to include may be

Twitter: twitter.com/brianjdixon

Blog: brianjdixon.com

Connect, Create, Contribute

A project-based, technology-infused high school located in downtown Baton Rouge.

Office hours: Available for parent conferences during third period (10:15 to 11:00 a.m.) each day and after school on Tuesdays and Thursdays.

Click here to make an appointment: <link to an online survey>.

ONGOING SOCIAL ENGAGEMENT WITH E-MAIL

You can use e-mail to help build ongoing social engagement with your school community (see Figure 8.6). Allowing you to do anything from building awareness through an emergency alert system to building collaboration through tracking e-mail threads, e-mail may be your favorite tool for communicating with members of your school community.

Awareness

E-mail is an incredible tool for building awareness. Simply write the content you would like to share, then type in the address of the person with whom you would

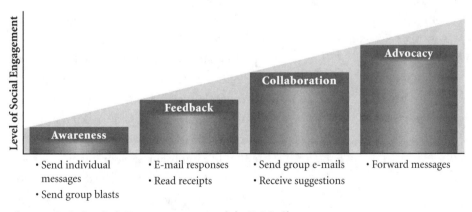

Figure 8.6 Social Engagement with E-Mail

At Ankeny High School, e-mail is used as part of the emergency alert system for parents. When an emergency occurs, the parents of over 1,700 students are contacted via e-mail and other media. Jarrett Peterson, district communication coordinator, explains that although emergency planning can sometimes feel like one more chore during a busy school day, "What is more important than the safety and security of students and staff?"

"Calm in the Face of Crisis," accessed April 22, 2012, http://thejournal.com/Articles /2011/04/06/Calm-in-the-Face-of-Crisis.aspx.

James Comer and Norris Haynes, professors at Yale University, believe that better lines of communication between home and school are vital to a student's success. E-mail as a method of communication can provide opportunities that perhaps would not otherwise be available. "Technology can allow educators and parents to be linked into a sturdier web of mutual support than ever before. Schools and homes can be connected through computer networks that allow them to freely share information, via e-mail and bulletin boards, twenty-four hours a day and year-round."

"The Home-School Team: An Emphasis on Parent Involvement," accessed December 3, 2011, www.edutopia.org/home-school-team.

like to share it, and he or she will instantly receive that content. This is the primary way e-mail is used: direct communication from one person to one or more other people.

Feedback

E-mail is of course a great tool for receiving direct feedback. Send a message to a specific person asking for his or her feedback, and you will probably receive a response. The more specific and targeted your request is, the more likely the recipient is to respond to your e-mail in a personalized way. Avoid sending the same message to more than one person. If you really need to—say you're asking the same question of your entire parent community or of more than one person—at least individually address the e-mail to each person. This can be done automatically using an eNewsletter service, through which the entire e-mail list is uploaded and then e-mails are sent out individually.

Collaboration

E-mail is also a great tool for building collaboration. Often the projects in which we participate as a school are a result of someone else's initiation, and this was probably done through e-mail. When I receive an e-mail from a parent or a teacher making a specific suggestion, it is easy for me to follow up, either by simply agreeing or by making slight modifications. Because most e-mail programs let you view conversations by subject, known as "threaded discussions," you can review the entire conversation across several e-mails, allowing you to continue moving the conversation forward, even in the middle of a busy day. This collaborative environment is one of the greatest benefits of using e-mail.

Advocacy

E-mail is also a dynamic tool for building advocacy online. Because forwarding a message is very simple, e-mail can be used to spread your message further. For example, you could send a short paragraph to your PTA parents expressing that this is an e-mail they could forward to other interested people. Include the paragraph in quotes so that they know to copy it and include it in their own personal e-mail. This will then be seen as a personalized message rather than a group blast.

COMMON SCHOOL TASKS BEFORE AND AFTER E-MAIL

E-mail can change the way you complete common school tasks, such as communicating changes to an event and sharing school-related messages.

Task or Goal	Traditional Method	Using E-Mail
Communicating an event's time change	Before e-mail, communicating a time change was very difficult, especially within twenty-four hours of the event. It was too late to send out a notification, and usually much too complicated to make a phone call to every recipient.	Sending an e-mail to your potential attendees notifying them of the time change is as simple as clicking a few buttons.
Sharing school-related messages	Before e-mail, it was nearly impossible for parents to share messages with their friends. You would ask for volunteers or request that parents remember to tell their friends and neighbors about an event happening at your school, but often this message was not passed on in the absence of a convenient tool such as e-mail.	With e-mail, parents can just forward that message, and parents and their friends can simply and easily be reminded of that message later when it's most important. The immediacy of e-mail enables personalized communication in profound ways.

GETTING STARTED WITH E-MAIL

Questions for Reflection: How many e-mails do you have waiting in your inbox right now? Of that total number, how many require your action? How many can be deleted? How many can be delegated to someone else? And how many can simply be archived, saved for future reference?

First Steps

1. Review the e-mail signatures of your teaching staff. Look for best practices and consider ways to encourage more professionalism.

2. Try emptying your inbox using the four-step e-mail processing plan given in this chapter. Post the results on your blog or Facebook profile.

CHAPTER 9

Classroom Portals

This chapter demonstrates how teachers can use classroom portals to enhance students' engagement in classroom learning. Topics covered in this chapter include

- Features of classroom portals
- Benefits of classroom portals
- Ongoing social engagement with classroom portals
- Common school tasks before and after classroom portals
- Tips for implementing classroom portals
- Getting started with classroom portals

Every class in your school should have an online portal, which is a place to which students can travel to virtually engage in classroom learning. Although the

Figure 9.1 Screenshot: Classroom Portal

portal may take the form of a blog, a course website, or a course management system, the approach is more engaging and collaborative. Rather than simply allowing students to download documents or access the teacher's e-mail address, a classroom portal allows a community of learners to interact with each other in authentic ways through such tools as document sharing, discussion forums, and commenting. For an example of a classroom portal, see Figure 9.1.

Multiple platforms, or online tools, exist that could serve as a classroom portal. From simple WordPress websites to detailed course management systems, such as Moodle or Blackboard, the technological tools available today are more plentiful than ever. For the sake of clarity, this chapter includes examples from the free, easy-to-use, and widely adopted Google Apps Suite, which includes Google Docs, Google Sites, Gmail, Google Calendar, Google+, and thousands of installable add-on applications through Google Apps Marketplace. Although these apps work together, this chapter will primarily focus on Google Sites as the basis of your classroom portal.

FEATURES OF CLASSROOM PORTALS

Online classroom portals, such as Google sites, are shareable pages online that allow students to access the classroom from anywhere that they can connect to the Internet. Common features of classroom portals include

- **Classroom information.** The teacher's contact information, the name of the class, an online syllabus, online textbooks or articles in pdf format, and links to relevant videos are all important components for students to be able to access. This information is easy to update with simple "edit" and "save" buttons.

- **Downloadable documents.** Anything that you photocopy and pass out to the class should be included as a downloadable link on your classroom portal. This includes permission forms, articles, worksheets, and even class notes. Archiving this important information will save you time in the future and will give students 24/7 access. This also makes it impossible for students to lose worksheets and notes.

- **Collaboration tools.** Transforming your classroom portal into a functional online community is dependent on frequent use of the available collaboration tools, including discussion forums, document uploading, commenting and rating features, screen sharing, and online chat tools.

- **Multimedia sharing.** From storing digital images of example work to housing video archives of classroom discussions, classroom portals allow simple uploading, viewing, and downloading of multimedia content to help extend the classroom environment beyond its physical walls.

- **User management.** User management enables the creation of both private and public pages, allowing limited viewing by public visitors and exclusive access to assignments, grades, and feedback for students and parents who have logged in online.

> *Kechia Williams, a sixth-grade language arts teacher in South Carolina, uses her classroom portal to keep parents informed about their child's performance at school. "Parents have to have an email address in order to access the system. Once signed in, they can see their child's progress, and recognize problem areas."*
>
> "Biography: Kechia Williams," accessed December 3, 2011, www.scholastic.com /teachers/contributor/kechia-williams.

BENEFITS OF CLASSROOM PORTALS

An online classroom portal has several benefits. These include enhanced access, enabled collaboration, authentic assessment, increased engagement, real-world relevance, and fewer photocopies.

Enhanced Access

Web-based classroom portals allow students to access the classroom 24/7 from wherever they are. Homework assignments left at school are no longer an excuse for incomplete work. Students can ask questions online, even after class has ended. They can also collaborate on group work from their own home.

Enabled Collaboration

Classroom portals change the dynamic of a class, with multiple users collaborating rather than one teacher delivering content. Teachers and students can quickly and easily update their profile, upload documents, and respond to others' work. Many tools, such as document sharing, allow groups to collaborate on a project in real time online. Students also benefit from the feedback they receive on their work from other students, helping shift the emphasis from the final grade they will receive to the quality of work they complete. This also helps students focus more on the process of completing work than on what the final product will look like.

Authentic Assessment

Rather than simply relying on a weekly test or homework as the main method of assessment, teachers can use a classroom portal to evaluate students using multiple means. A discussion forum rubric can be useful in assessing constructive contributions that students have made to the class. Revision tracking helps educators evaluate progress in students' writing projects. Online pre- and posttests allow students to demonstrate mastery of key classroom concepts.

Increased Engagement

With a classroom portal, multiple conversations can occur at the same time. Instead of having every student individually complete the same assignment, a classroom portal allows students to build on one another's work. In one central location, students can respond to the classroom discussion, write their thoughts on the assigned class reading, and give feedback on the original work of their peers. Expressing their own viewpoint and hearing those of other students increases students' engagement in the course activities. The classroom portal also creates a safe space for students to share their thoughts; some students who may be too shy to participate in the classroom will feel more comfortable engaging online.

> *Nicholas Provenzano, an English teacher at Grosse Pointe South High School in Michigan, highly recommends both using classroom portals to organize course content and making this content engaging and interactive by bringing it online. "It has not only freed up time and space in my room, but also made for some great opportunities for student engagement."*
>
> "Summer PD: Use a Web Site to Help Manage Your Classroom," posted August 9, 2011, www.edutopia.org/blog/use-the-web-for-classroom-management-nick-provenzano.

Real-World Relevance

Because the classroom portal can be updated by anyone, anywhere, what used to be static classroom content can now be made increasingly more relevant. When a story breaks in the news, links to the story and related videos can be posted on the classroom portal. Students can respond to these resources, allowing them to engage in the ongoing conversation that the adult world is having. These activities help make course content and state standards more relevant to students, demonstrating a link between their classroom learning and the world around them.

> **Tip**   One real-world skill that classroom portals can help facilitate is scheduling meetings. Using the integrated calendar feature in Google Apps, students can learn to make appointments with each other and their teachers. Encouraging students to use their own Google calendar will help them learn time management and planning.

Fewer Photocopies

Classroom portals effectively save paper and time. Downloadable forms created in Word can be posted on the classroom portal for parents to download and print at their convenience. Google Docs prevents printing needless papers because students can complete their worksheets individually online. They can "share" documents with the teacher so that he or she can check their work without printing out a paper copy. Classroom portals essentially serve as online document repositories, increasing communication with parents and preventing headaches caused by students' losing take-home packets.

ONGOING SOCIAL ENGAGEMENT WITH CLASSROOM PORTALS

A classroom portal is a dynamic tool to increase your school's ongoing social engagement (see Figure 9.2). It allows you to build awareness, lets students give and receive feedback, fosters collaboration with the school community, and helps you empower your community members to advocate for your school.

Awareness

Classroom portals allow educators to share information with students and parents about assignments, upcoming tests, and classroom content. A classroom portal can be used to post homework, news, and upcoming events.

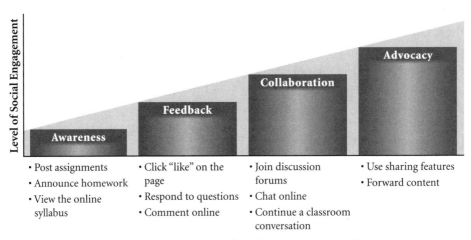

Figure 9.2 Social Engagement with Classroom Portals

Feedback

Classroom portals allow participants to receive feedback from their school community. Visitors are able to give their direct feedback, whether they are responding by clicking on an e-mail link, clicking a "like" button to acknowledge something that's been posted, or writing a text comment on an item posted in the classroom portal.

Collaboration

Various elements of a classroom portal, including discussion forums and online chat tools, enable educators to collaborate with parents and students by engaging in an ongoing conversation online.

Advocacy

The sharing features built into classroom portals allow parents and students to spread classroom content and information beyond the walls of the classroom and into their own networks. Sharing content from a classroom portal with contacts outside of the school through social networks helps inform the community about exciting projects and programs at the school. This sharing furthers the reach of the school community, building buzz and challenging others to support and participate in ongoing activities.

> A recent survey in Edutopia found that online classroom portals were one of parents' top choices for means of staying in contact with their child's school. Offering registered parent accounts that allow parents to keep track of grades and stay in touch with teachers was particularly appreciated by the parents surveyed.
>
> "What Parents Want in School Education," posted August 31, 2011, www.edutopia.org /blog/parent-involvement-survey-anne-obrien.

> According Elizabeth Delmatoff, a seventh-grade technology teacher in Portland, Oregon, "Working with students creating blogs and online journals has been a wonderful activity to connect and collaborate with students. . . . It has allowed me insight into my students' lives. We have been able to participate in group discussions based on their writings, and utilize collaborative and peer teaching methods."
>
> "The Benefits of Blogging for Kids," accessed April 23, 2012, http://edsome.com/2010/11 /the-benefits-of-blogging-for-kids/.

COMMON SCHOOL TASKS BEFORE AND AFTER CLASSROOM PORTALS

Online classroom portals can change the way teachers complete common school tasks, such as distributing forms for parents, communicating assignments, handling student absences, facilitating student presentations, and scheduling parent conferences.

Task or Goal	Traditional Method	Using Classroom Portals
Handing out and collecting field trip forms	Traditionally, teachers would create a field trip packet on the computer, print it, photocopy it, staple it, and hand it out to every student. If they were to lose it, the teacher would give them another copy, have copies available at the office, or make copies from another student's packet.	With Google Docs, teachers can create the document online, save it, and make it accessible to anyone who has the link, the password, or an e-mail sharing the document. They can edit it if the document creator allows students to fill out the form online. Teachers can automatically collect the details online or on their phone, and student packets can be instantly printed. These data can never be lost because they are constantly backed up and saved.
Communicating homework assignments	Teachers might assign homework to students, have them write the assignment in their agenda, and have it initialed by a parent. But some students would never write down the homework. Others would forget to bring their agenda home; they would leave class with the homework written down, but would leave their agenda in the hallway, in their locker, on the bus, at a friend's house, or anywhere else other than their home.	Teachers can create a homework page on the classroom portal to post to daily. Before leaving each day, they can click "edit," type out the homework, and add it at the top so that assignments are in reverse chronological order—starting with the newest at the top. Students simply have to visit the classroom portal's homework page to view the assignments. Teachers can even track who viewed the page.

Task or Goal	Traditional Method	Using Classroom Portals
Handling student absences	Before classroom portals, students who were out sick could not participate in the day's classroom activities. They therefore had to wait until they returned to school to learn about what they missed.	Students can create a homework wiki using classroom portals. Here's how it works. Teachers don't have to do anything. Students fill in the wiki and can ask questions. All contributors are logged by time and username, and edits are password protected. Students take responsibility for their homework and can add to the classroom portal to complete assignments. This allows students who are out sick to access the classroom content, ask questions, and post feedback. This all ensures that these students do not fall behind while out of school.
Facilitating student presentations	Students would schedule a time in class to present their assignment. They might show a PowerPoint presentation to the class and be graded by the teacher. Parents would be invited to attend, but they had to be physically present.	The student makes a presentation to the class using the Google Docs version of PowerPoint. Parents can log on to the presentation online and can even participate in real time.

(continued)

Task or Goal	Traditional Method	Using Classroom Portals
Scheduling parent conferences	Parents would call the school or send a note to the teacher requesting a parent conference. It could take a few days to have the conference scheduled, with phone calls back and forth.	If using Google Sites to manage the classroom portal, for example, educators can embed a Google calendar. Posting a Google calendar allows students, parents, and others to visit the portal to check the teacher's availability or to look at other appointments that have been set. There are several ways to use a classroom portal to make appointments: by clicking to e-mail a meeting request; by using a form, such as one generated by Wufoo or Google; or by using a collaborative meeting scheduler, such as Doodle.

TIPS FOR IMPLEMENTING CLASSROOM PORTALS

Encouraging teachers to create and manage their classroom portals can seem like an overwhelming task for some school administrators. Although classroom portals clearly have advantages over traditional systems for organizing classroom information, there may be additional challenges that teachers face. Here are a few best practices to help minimize and mitigate these potential problems:

Use a Widely Adopted Tool

This is one of my main reasons for suggesting that teachers and school administrators embrace Google Apps as their chosen platform for classroom portals. There is no bigger tool out there. Google has a vast wealth of training resources available online. Plus, it is very intuitive, even for the most technophobic users. Creating a new page is as simple as clicking "new," typing the information, and clicking "save." It's that easy.

Share Best Practices

One of the strategies that has worked well in the school I have worked with is creating opportunities to share best practices. Teachers should have a space to take what they know and share it with others. The more accessible the content, the more people might use it. Encourage teachers to share their best practices through technology luncheons, training opportunities, and online classroom portals. Frequently sharing best practices can have a tremendous impact on teachers' embracing the tools they have available to them. If a seasoned colleague can update his or her own website, it demonstrates that the average classroom teacher can do the same.

Offer Training Resources

Purchase a book on Google Apps, and hold a faculty training session to share what you learned from the book. Training resources can also be found and shared for free online. Administrators can send teachers a list of links to videos and online articles to help teachers better use these tools.

Evaluate Implementation

What gets measured gets managed. When teachers know that administrators will be following up with them and assessing how they are using the tools given to them, they will take using classroom portals much more seriously. If possible, tie their use of classroom portals to their performance indicators.

"I use Google Sites for my website for my students. On that website I write 'blog' posts every day where I tell what lesson we did that day and any class work I assigned," explains Julia Hill, a math teacher at Worcester Technical High School in Newark, Maryland. *"If a student is absent and has access to the Internet they can try to make up their work before they come back. I also post pdf files of their homework packet so if they lose it they don't have to ask me for a new one. They can just print one from home."*

"Frustration Abounds!" posted February 24, 2011, http://wthshill.edublogs.org/2011/02/24/.

Edutopia contributing writer Sara Ring suggests using a classroom portal, in this case a blog, to post information about upcoming events, lessons, and assignments. "You can easily update and edit it from anywhere. Your students can create their own blogs to display writing and photos and to share information with each other. And you can set all blogs to 'private' so only those users you approve may access them."

"Google for Educators: The Best Features for Busy Teachers," accessed December 3, 2011, www.edutopia.org/google-for-educators.

Include updating the classroom portal as part of their formal observation. Posting lesson plans and objectives online can be a key component of teachers' observation rubric. There is simply no excuse for not using the effective tools now available, especially with so many training resources to help teachers get comfortable with these new technologies.

GETTING STARTED WITH CLASSROOM PORTALS

Question for Reflection: What are your current expectations for teachers in regard to the online posting of homework?

First Steps

1. Form a classroom portal committee, requesting feedback from teachers about what should be required of a classroom portal.

2. Sign up for Google Apps and try using Google Sites to create an online portal. Focus on one topic, such as faculty meeting agendas or parent-teacher communication ideas. Share what you learned in the process with your classroom portal committee.

3. Visit the websites of other schools to see how they have embraced classroom portals as a method for increasing community engagement. Reach out to model schools for advice and guidance.

Student Portfolios

Online student portfolios are websites that allow students to showcase their best work for the community to see. These are often hosted on a blog platform, such as WordPress, or on Google Sites. These sites feature editing tools that allow students to quickly and easily update and edit their pages and content. Students use online portfolios to post their work online, reflect on their learning experiences, share career goals, and express themselves.

Student portfolios help students apply the ongoing social engagement model to their own practice. They help students engage the community, including other students, parents, teachers, colleges, and employers. This chapter outlines the following topics:

- Features of student portfolios

- Why use student portfolios?

- Best practices for student portfolios

- Technology tips for student portfolios
- Ongoing social engagement with student portfolios
- Getting started with student portfolios

FEATURES OF STUDENT PORTFOLIOS

Student portfolios can include anything that reflects the student's work, personality, and academic interests. They most often include the following elements:

"About Me" Page

This page is an opportunity for students to express themselves on their student portfolio. They can write a description about who they are, include a short biography, include a link to an online résumé, state their learning goals, and link to their social media profiles. Often this page includes a picture of the student (see Figure 10.1 for an example).

Students' Best Work

A key component of an online student portfolio is student-created work. When students highlight their best work on their online portfolio, this can impress the

Figure 10.1 Screenshot: Student Portfolio

portfolio viewer. Examples of student work include projects, papers, and presentations:

- **Projects.** These are often documented on student portfolios through pictures and descriptions of the project. Projects allow viewers to see examples of original student thought. Viewers get to see each student's creativity and learn about his or her work ethic and design process.

- **Papers.** These are often posted in a sharable format, for example as pdf files, allowing the portfolio viewer to read, download, and print student writing. Online papers help showcase students' writing voice and ability. Featured papers might include a mix of fiction; narrative nonfiction; reports; and practical papers, such as college admissions essays or life statements.

- **Presentations.** These are often shared in an embedded PowerPoint format, allowing students to display their best work in a collaborative way and to summarize what they have been working on. Video files of these presentations can also help the audience get to know students and their presentation skills.

Learning Goals

Student portfolios often include students' learning goals. Posting learning goals is a way for students to share their ambitions and their personality.

Online Résumé

Often the student portfolio has elements of an online résumé, including work and volunteer experience, academic achievements, and any awards that students want to share online.

WHY USE STUDENT PORTFOLIOS?

Online student portfolios hold several advantages for both the students and your school as a whole. This section outlines eleven reasons to consider implementing student portfolios at your school.

The National Education Technology Plan, a collaborative effort of the U.S. Department of Education and seventeen leading educators from across the nation, explains that student portfolios can "help students develop the self-awareness required to set their own learning goals, express their own views of their strengths, weaknesses, and achievements, and take responsibility for them."

"What 21st Century Learning Should Look Like," accessed December 3, 2011, www.ed.gov/technology/draft-netp-2010/what-21st-century-learning-should-look-like.

- **Help students with college acceptance.** Student portfolios go beyond SAT scores, ACT scores, GPAs, and college entrance essays. College admissions counselors love to look at student portfolios. They give them a more well-rounded perspective on the contributions that each student could make to the university campus. Student portfolios that have been created and curated over several years provide a unique perspective and a transparent glimpse into students' personality and work ethic, helping students demonstrate what sets them apart from their peers.

> Jessie Thaler, a classroom teacher at Claremont Middle School in North Oakland, explains, "I think that eighth graders are at the age where they really need authentic reasons to write, and they really need motivation. A blog is a way to see work in print and have a truly authentic purpose. It means that people other than their teacher will be reading their work."
>
> "Blogs Give Students an Audience," posted January 13, 2009, www.edutopia.org/blog-teaching.

- **Serve as a great complement to their résumé.** Employers and managers of internships love student portfolios because they get a sense of who the student really is beyond just his or her schoolwork. This allows them to see volunteerism, activities, hobbies, interests, and skills.

- **Keep students engaged at your school.** When schools use student portfolios they see an increased level of student engagement. Student work becomes more valuable when students know that someone other than their teacher will be viewing it. When students are able to choose their best work to share with the larger community, they put forth greater effort in producing a quality final product.

- **Help students set goals for achievement and personal development.** The student portfolio is also a great place for a student to create and share goals for specific achievements and personal development. The social pressure of posting a goal online can have a great impact on a student's achieving that goal.

- **Let students quickly and easily post their best work using familiar tools.** Portfolio platforms, such as Google Sites, allow students to keep portfolios updated with simple posting, sharing, and saving features. What once required complex Web programming is now as easy as saving a Word document. This ease of use allows students to focus on creating high-quality content for their portfolio instead of on the tools and programming that were once required.

- **Allow students to challenge their peers.** When students are able to actually view the work of their peers, they are often inspired to reach higher, dig deeper, and work harder than ever before. Educators can use this peer pressure in a positive way to encourage students to create their best work. Students, by sharing their portfolio with their peers, challenge each other to create more interesting and engaged portfolios.

- **Let students collaborate on assignments.** Students can use a tool such as Google Sites to edit each other's work. By integrating Google Docs with their online portfolio, students can work together to create and edit their projects, presentations, and papers. This means that a group project truly becomes a group project, with all members of the group having an opportunity to add their own perspective and content to that collaborative effort.

- **Serve as a great place for student expression.** One of the most overlooked yet valuable reasons to have students use online portfolios is to offer a place for student expression. The online portfolio can be a fascinating medium for students to share their unique talents and individual personalities. Digital tools allow student portfolios to be highly customized, with students changing the background colors, adding pictures, and modifying the design to better express their identity. Challenge students to keep the audience in mind and to balance personal expression with clear communication.

- **Are an excellent student recruiting tool.** When prospective students visit your school website and see high-quality student portfolios, those upcoming students will be inspired, imagining themselves in the shoes of a current student. Posting links to student portfolios on your website can help prospective students be better informed about the experience that your school provides and enable them to see the kind of work they would create if they were to attend your school.

- **Act as an alternative assessment to yield authentic, real-world feedback.** Posting student work on a portfolio allows for authentic assessment. Evaluating student performance based on multiple measures is an effective way to give students feedback and to assess their skill development. Beyond assigning a simple letter grade for a finished piece, you get to see what a student actually learned by viewing multiple iterations of a project as well as students' own reflections on their work. In an age of high-stakes testing, many educators have moved away from most forms of alternative assessment. Student portfolios are very "real world" in that they require planning, writing, revising, and publishing, and they garner feedback from multiple sources. As we prepare our students for the knowledge economy, their online portfolio may just be the best tool we have given them to use.

- **Help students learn media literacy skills.** The key skill for students in this digital age is learning how to find and respond to great content to make it part of their story. They should not be information gatherers or collectors, but rather users or synthesizers of information. The process of creating and updating an online portfolio gives students the opportunity to develop the media literacy skills they need to be globally competitive.

BEST PRACTICES FOR STUDENT PORTFOLIOS

Here are some best practices to help students use student portfolios:

Have a Planned Rollout

When launching an online student portfolio program, follow a planned procedure that includes training; setting expectations; monitoring student content; and specifying the frequency with which students will post and update content, give and receive feedback, and undergo assessment.

Attend to Frequency Concerns

One of the keys to using student portfolios is frequently attending to the following elements:

- **Posting.** Portfolios are a work in progress. Outdated content can quickly lead to disengagement by the portfolio viewer and the student creator. Make updating student portfolios part of the weekly class schedule.

- **Presentation.** Hold students accountable for updating their respective online portfolios by having each student present his or her portfolio once a month to the class. Students should have something new to share each time they present.

- **Feedback.** Allow other students to give their feedback and suggestions. Rotate students through a daily portfolio presentation, with one student updating the class on his or her portfolio progress each and every day. This way they can all regularly give and receive feedback.

- **Assessment.** Create a schoolwide rubric to set clear expectations for student portfolios. Uniform guidelines will help ensure student portfolios are of the highest quality.

> *According to Helen Barrett, an adjunct faculty member in educational technology at Seattle Pacific University, "One of the most effective uses of a portfolio is to review a learner's work and provide feedback for improvement."*
>
> "Processes," accessed April 29, 2012, http://electronicportfolios.org/academy/mportfolios/home/processes/index.html.

Address Plagiarism

The ease of sharing, accessing, copying, and pasting content may tempt students to plagiarize material in their online portfolio. Here are two tools to help stop the plagiarism.

- **Turnitin.** Turnitin is a great program used by schools—universities, colleges, and high schools—across the country. Students submit the assignment to Turnitin, and that system automatically looks for plagiarism, checks to see that citations are in APA or MLA style, and provides a report. The teacher can put more focus on what the students are learning rather than on how they are presenting it.

- **Google Search.** Another easy way of checking for plagiarism, especially if it is a specific sentence that stands out in the paper, is to use Google. Take the whole sentence, put quotation marks around it, plug it into Google, and do a search. It will search all of the websites in the entire world that have been indexed by Google for that specific phrase. A more organized way to do this is with Dupli Checker, which will take a long passage; break it into segments; and perform thirty Google, Bing, or Yahoo searches at one time. These searches can be done with quotes to find exact plagiarism and without quotes to find paraphrasing. If Google finds the information somewhere, then it is a good time for the teacher to talk to the student about the ethical use of resources.

TECHNOLOGY TIPS FOR STUDENT PORTFOLIOS

Implementing online student portfolios on a schoolwide basis can be a daunting task for even the most experienced faculty team. These three technology tips will help ensure an effective student portfolio program.

- **Choose function over fashion.** Although there are more professional platforms, such as WordPress and Drupal, our school uses Google Sites for our online portfolio system. Google Sites is easy to use and has many templates to get you started. With simple tools like Google Sites, students can readily update their portfolio with recent work without extensive tech knowledge.

- **Leverage training resources.** No matter what system you use, ensure that students have access to training resources. With Google Sites, many students will be able to get started without any technology training. Google Sites and WordPress do have training tools available online, including video tutorials, forums, and user guides, for when a student needs help or wants to explore advanced features.

- **Manage users.** When implementing an online portfolio system, ensure that you are able to perform basic administrative functions. From our experience, you will need to frequently register new users, remove inappropriate content, and reset user passwords. Instead of having students sign up for a website of which you're not an administrator, such as Webs (webs.com) or WordPress, you can have them use Google Sites, which allows you to perform administrative functions across your school network.

ONGOING SOCIAL ENGAGEMENT WITH STUDENT PORTFOLIOS

Student portfolios can help build ongoing social engagement online—engagement with the school and with the students themselves (see Figure 10.2). From sharing their projects online to build awareness to participating in collaborative projects, students can use online portfolios in ways that lead to a deeper level of engagement for the entire school community.

Awareness

Student portfolios can be a great tool for building awareness about your school as well as the learning activities in which your students are participating. A blog

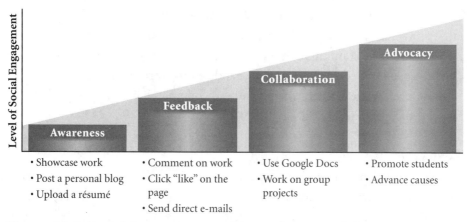

- Showcase work
- Post a personal blog
- Upload a résumé

- Comment on work
- Click "like" on the page
- Send direct e-mails

- Use Google Docs
- Work on group projects

- Promote students
- Advance causes

Figure 10.2 Social Engagement with Student Portfolios

section on the portfolio would allow students to share news and updates with the community. Another way to build awareness is to share student projects online, and the student portfolio is the perfect place to highlight the best student work. Making these pages available to the public and linking to student portfolios from your website will enable Web visitors to learn more about the day-to-day classroom activities at your school. This will help inform parents, potential students, and community members about the exciting learning experiences that your students encounter daily.

Feedback

Student portfolios allow students to receive helpful feedback from the school community. Students who post projects on their online portfolio can receive authentic feedback from teachers, peers, parents, and, depending on sharing preferences, the greater community. As an example, a student who writes an essay on a local issue, such as water quality in the area, can post it as a blog entry on his student portfolio and then share the link with the local city council or the water district officials. Comments can be posted directly onto the blog, or the student could receive replies to the e-mail address associated with his student account.

Collaboration

Online portfolios can enhance the collaboration occurring at your school by enabling students to have ongoing conversations with their peers, teachers, and community members. Student portfolios can also be used to collaborate with other students, artists, or professionals. This can occur by receiving blog comments from these community members, using an embedded version of Google Docs to collaboratively edit documents, and setting portfolio editing preferences to allow a wiki-style format, whereby other people can edit the student portfolio and add their own feedback.

Advocacy

The sharing features of student portfolios encourage the promotion of student work. Say, for example, a student has designed a poster advocating for higher-water quality in the local area. This work can reach a larger audience by being posted on another website, shared through e-mail, or distributed on a social network, such as Facebook. All of the shares and posts can lead back to the student blog, helping it receive more visitors. The student can be seen as an advocate for the social cause, and perhaps will even be interviewed by the local media to talk about the passion he has for this cause. This moves the learning experience from the four walls of the classroom out into the community, and it can have a dramatic impact on the learning experiences of students.

GETTING STARTED WITH STUDENT PORTFOLIOS

Question for Reflection: In your opinion, why should students create and maintain their own online portfolio?

First Steps

1. Contact two or three college admissions counselors (no matter what grade level you work at). Ask for their opinion about online portfolios.

2. Reach out to a group of students to pilot a student portfolio program.

School Leader's Blog

Your school community wants to hear from you as the leader of the school. They want to know what is happening at the school and understand your vision for where the school is headed. In an age of Twitter and podcasting, weekly newsletters are no longer good enough. School leaders need to use today's technology to accomplish the authentic communication expected in our connected world. A key platform you can use to communicate with your school community is a school leader's blog.

This chapter demonstrates the importance of a professional blog for the innovative school leader. Citing examples from the field, this chapter will teach you how to use the latest blogging tools to build social engagement into your professional practice. Chapter highlights include

- What is a blog?

- Why use a blog?

- Finding topics to write about
- Finding time to blog
- Features of your blogging platform
- Building your platform
- Best practices for blogging
- Ongoing social engagement with a school leader's blog
- Common school tasks before and after starting a blog
- Getting started with your blog

WHAT IS A BLOG?

A blog is an online journal of ideas. It is a website that is updated with new content frequently, whether daily or weekly. Blogs can take many different forms, including video, audio, text, and multimedia. Blogs are free to create and publish. They are hosted on a server where the content is saved. You log on to your blog; type your new content with a title and body text, often including multimedia or a picture; and then click "publish." In less than a minute you can have a professional looking blog that is online and viewable to anyone in the world. Blogs feature advanced functions that enable you to

- Track view statistics
- Record which entries are being shared the most
- Create a custom design for a personalized look and feel
- Update content from a mobile device

What makes a blog social is that there are many sharing features that take it beyond just viewing, printing, or reading articles. Let's say, for example, that you write a post about a unique classroom management strategy that you have seen to be effective at your school. You explain the strategy in your blog post, include a few examples, and then send it to the Web by posting it on your blog. Other school leaders and teachers read this blog post, like your suggestions, and want to share your content with their network.

Blog platforms also can include plug-ins that will allow your blog to do more than just serve as an online journal of ideas. These plug-ins allow your blog to

- Be easily read using a mobile application on a phone
- Appear more like a photo album than a newspaper
- Be read aloud with an audio program

With thousands of plug-ins available and blog developers around the world, blogs are only limited by your imagination and the content you create.

WHY USE A BLOG?

There are many reasons to create and keep an updated blog. As a school leader, your primary goals are most likely to promote your school and share your professional ideas. Specific reasons to blog about your thoughts include the following:

Casting a Leadership Vision

You set the tone and cast the vision—for your students, your staff, your parents, and the larger community around your school. What you feel is important is what will be seen as important. You set the priorities. You have the natural platform to communicate your leadership vision.

- What is the vision of your school?
- In which direction are you headed?
- How do local and national events affect your students?

Your school community wants to hear your perspective on these issues.

Sharing Your School's Story

Every school has a brand, an image that is being projected into the community. People are continually adding to the story of your school, but there is no better representative than the school leader. People look for guidance and direction in telling the story of their school. In many ways, you *are* your school's brand because the school leader is the chief representative of a school's mission and message. See figure 11.1 for an example of a school leader's blog.

> *Eric Sheninger, principal of New Milford High School in New Jersey, remarks that blogging "creates a layer of transparency and gives stakeholders a glimpse into what I do, how I think, and what I am passionate about."*
>
> "The Social Media Conundrum," posted May 4, 2011, www.connectedprincipals.com /archives/3491.

Figure 11.1 Screenshot: School Leader's Blog

Influencing the Educational Community

The lessons you learn as a school leader deserve a larger audience than your single school. Your school community is a living, learning lab, and the solutions that you experiment with, create, and test can have an impact on others at your school, in your local district, and across the nation. Not sharing your best practices is a missed opportunity to participate in improving the education system at large. You no longer have to wait for publication in an education journal or to speak at a conference to see your ideas influence other schools. You can now share your ideas directly with other principals through a post on your blog. You can link to this content through your Twitter feed, Facebook page, or school website for other school leaders to read, no matter where they live or when they happen to find the content.

Improving your Professional Practice

Another reason to keep a blog is to reflect on and improve your practice. When you take the time to process and consider your experiences—what worked and what didn't, what went well and what could be improved—you become a reflective leader. You will be able to look back on blog posts from previous school years and receive encouragement from the challenges you lived through and learned from. You can use what you experience each day to become a better leader, to share your ideas with others, and to empower your school community. Your blog serves as an ongoing record of your professional experience over time.

Growing Your Platform and Career

Building a following for your blog can help you reach a global audience. One blog post on a relevant topic that makes an impression on a reader can be shared with an audience that you have never before engaged. A superintendent of a large school district could read your blog post and then send it to his or her school principals, who then read it and send it to their teachers and their colleagues in other school districts.

All of this can happen in a matter of minutes. No longer do you have to wait to write an article; submit it for publication to multiple magazines with a sixty- to ninety-day lead time; wait several months for the article to come out; and then have only those who have paid to receive the magazine read the article, be influenced by it, photocopy it, and share it with others. Instead, all of this is done with a click of a button and strokes on a keyboard.

FINDING TOPICS TO WRITE ABOUT

One of the advantages of being a school leader who is beginning to blog is that there is never a shortage of topics to write about. This being said, some first-time bloggers have trouble getting started. Remember that your school community cares what you think about and will think about what you care about. Your students, teachers, parents, and community want to hear your viewpoint on a variety of topics. These include such items as your thoughts on students using Facebook, best practices for classroom management, what the ideal lesson plan looks like, how to have the perfect parent meeting, and other best practices that you have learned in your many years of teaching and leadership. Eventually your well of ideas will run dry. You will run out of topics to share, and you will need to find other sources of inspiration. This section provides several sources of topic ideas to help your blog become a must-visit place online.

Frequently Asked Questions

A great place to find blog topics is frequently asked questions. Start with questions you are often asked by teachers, parents, and students. There are also many places online where people post questions to which they are searching for answers. By starting with a question that has already been asked on another site, you can use this content in several places. First create your own blog post, and then cross-post your answer on the site where the question was originally asked. Your post will continue to be read by future visitors looking for answers to that same question.

The Local News

As the head of your school, you can engage in the community conversation by writing about and responding to local news that affects your students, your school, and your community. You can comment on what happens in your local community, whether the topic of discussion is a new local ordinance, a recent crime, or an upcoming community event. Consider the impact of that news story on your school community, including your students, teachers, and parents. Write a short post on the topic (five hundred words will do) that incorporates your summary of the story, a few thoughts on the story's impact, and a link back to the original news story online. After you've posted your content on your blog, visit the comment section of the news article online and post a snippet of your content there with a link to your blog site. Depending on the news article, you might even send a link to the reporter

> *Norman Maynard, principal of Thornton Friends Upper School, says of his blog, "I talk about what's going on in school, upcoming events, school philosophy, adolescent health tips, and so on, while offering discussion forums, an image gallery, a calendar, and, in the near future, a link to an online bookstore."*
>
> "Sage Advice: What's the Best Way to Stay Connected to Parents?" accessed December 3, 2011, www.edutopia.org/groups/edutopia-welcome-lounge/14937.

> *To help build your personal brand online, author Gary Vaynerchuk recommends thinking of at least fifty awesome blog topics in your field to write about. He goes further, stating, "I'm convinced that if something is your true passion you can find five hundred things—five hundred interesting things—to say about it."*
>
> Gary Vaynerchuk, *Crush It! Why NOW Is the Time to Cash In on Your Passion* (New York: HarperBusiness, 2009), 50.

with your blog post. Make a habit of creating high-quality posts on local issues, and in due time that reporter will begin looking to you as a reference and an expert on future stories.

The National News

National news sources provide excellent, content-specific blog topics. Such publications as the *New York Times,* the *Washington Post,* and *Education Week* provide interesting fodder for blogs by reporting on topics of national importance. Your blog can provide examples in practice for a theoretical article or a local perspective on a national issue. The key to using local and national news as content for your blog is timeliness—you want to ensure that your blog is seen as a response to the article, posted within a few hours of the original content. Post your response to the page on which the article appears on the *New York Times* website, for example. Readers of the *New York Times* are probably much greater in number than those who frequently visit your site, and therefore those who read your comment and find it fascinating are likely to click the link to your site to see what more you have to say. This will help you to gain more readers because many news sites that allow for comments also allow you to post links back to your blog. Include an invitation to visit your blog at the end of every comment you post and you are likely to see your blog's audience numbers begin to grow.

> *Ann Hadley, chief content officer for MarketingProfs, suggests that you "take a stand about something; become a linchpin for discussion around the topic."*
>
> "How to Increase Social Sharing to Generate More Leads," posted December 12, 2011, www.entrepreneur.com/article/220720.

Other Blogs

Another great place to find topics to blog about is on other education-focused blogs. To find similar blogs, just google "top education blogs." The results will display several sites with updated lists of the most popular education blogs. Skim through the blog descriptions and choose three to five blogs to follow. Many will have invitations for interaction, including an opportunity to enter your e-mail address to subscribe or receive updates. Fill out these forms to learn how the best blogs keep their readers engaged. When a topic that is relevant to you arrives in your inbox, respond to the blog post on that site, and also post your comment on your own site with additional questions, comments, or resources to add to the ongoing discussion. Give people a reason to visit your site.

> **Tip** Ensure that you are contributing to the conversation and not just advertising your blog. Most blog platforms allow approval and deletion of comments. So, if your comment is on topic and adds to the quality of the conversation, it will probably be approved, even if your comment is critical of the blog post to which you are responding.

Quotes

Another strategy for finding blog topics is starting with quotes. There are websites and books that collect quotations by famous authors, politicians, and thought leaders from the past and the present day. Commenting on John Dewey, for example, will connect you with other educational leaders who embrace the Deweyan approach, helping to establish you as a leader in that particular discipline. Your leadership status could lead to consulting opportunities, speaking engagements, book sales, and further recognition in your field.

> **Advanced Tip** A great way to discover new quotes is by using Amazon's Most Highlighted Passages feature (see Figure 11.2). Just visit kindle.amazon.com, search for a topic in which you are interested and click on the book that appears. Below the description of the book you will find a collection of the most popular passages other readers have highlighted in the Kindle version of that book.

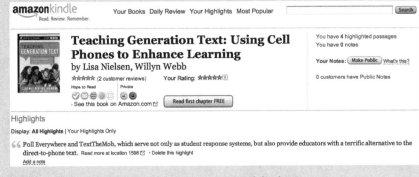

Figure 11.2 Screenshot: Amazon Highlights

Idea Websites

Because so many people are posting blogs and running out of content, there are many websites dedicated to blog ideas and topic suggestions. One great site to check out is Alltop, which features only the top articles from many of the leading websites. Responding to these articles is a great way to drive traffic to your site. You might also consider subscribing to Need a Topic, a weekly e-mail service that sends you five to ten blog topic ideas and useful tips for growing your blog.

Trending Topics

Twitter is a great website for learning about what people are currently talking about. Twitter's homepage features trending topics, highlighting the ten most popular topics on Twitter at a given moment. This feature not only tells you what people are talking about but also serves as a great place to find ideas for blog posts. These ideas can be great starting points for creating content that people care about. You can capitalize on a trending topic that is in your field and can quickly become the go-to expert on a topic in which others are actively interested.

An effective blog has high-quality, timely, and relevant content posted frequently enough to keep readers coming back. Here are a few more ideas to give you topics to write about:

- **Host an interactive book talk.** One day a week, write about a book you are currently reading. You might consider starting a book club to help you stay on track and interact with other school leaders reading the same book.

- **Make announcements.** Use your blog to post updates and announcements. The unlimited space on your blog affords you the opportunity to present your perspective on school decisions, allowing visitors to understand the backstory. Often hearing the longer explanation or the reason behind a difficult decision can help turn adversaries into allies.

- **Reflect on past events.** Write about your experiences as a school leader in the style of a memoir, sharing lessons learned and suggestions for up-and-coming leaders.

- **Share best practices.** Consider sharing the best tips that you have learned in your years of experience working in schools. These topics may include tips for new teachers, suggestions for how parents can help their child with homework, effective PTA strategies, technology tips, and ideas for preparing for the first day of school.

Before Going Public

Before telling the world about your blog, follow these simple guidelines:

1. **Develop a writing routine and content schedule.** Successful bloggers determine and follow an "editorial calendar" with content planned for specific days.

2. **Write three to five posts to help develop your writing voice.** It often takes a few tries to determine your voice and intended audience. Rewrite or make private the posts that don't match your style.

3. **Schedule your posts.** Instead of writing and immediately posting content, use the scheduling function to determine when new content will appear. Work a few posts ahead and allow content to build up. Conduct ongoing research to help you stay on schedule and not disappoint your readers. It's amazing how many people begin a blog, tell everyone they know, and then never update it again.

4. **Seek immediate feedback.** After posting three to five articles, send an e-mail to a few trusted colleagues soliciting their feedback. Their perspective and suggestions can greatly improve your blog before it reaches a larger audience.

5. **Ignore visitor statistics.** It can be very tempting to track every page visit and link click. For the first six months to a year, just focus on writing and publishing great content. People naturally find excellent content online. Concentrate on writing and sharing, and you'll begin to build a loyal audience over time.

FINDING TIME TO BLOG

One of the biggest challenges school leaders face in writing their blog is keeping it updated. There is always more work to do, and there's never enough time for daily tasks, let alone for thinking about and writing a blog. The urgent often overshadows the important. Finding time to write and reflect on a regular basis will not only improve your professional practice but also help you build a platform that opens you up to career advancement opportunities. Don't let the urgency of now distract you from the strategic building of tomorrow. Here are a few ideas that might help you squeeze out a few minutes from each day to keep your blog current.

Use Your Morning Commute

Because you already need to drive to school every day, use your commute as an opportune time to work on writing your blog. Use the voice recording app on your mobile device to record your thoughts, ideas, and reflections. Transcribing this audio is easy with many transcription programs available for your computer. The Dragon Dictation app automatically transcribes your voice recording on the go. Although it is limited to one minute of audio per recording, it is a convenient option for quickly recording and sharing your ideas. After your voice recording is transcribed, you can click the "share" button within the app to instantly post this content onto your blog. You might also consider hiring a transcription service online, with some charging just a few cents per minute of audio. These services even edit your content for clarity, and the transcriptions are usable as blog content without much editing. Better using your commute will help you generate blog content on a regular basis.

Establish a Daily Routine

Don't check your e-mail until 8:30 in the morning. One of the ways I found time to write this book while in the midst of leading two schools was by getting into the office an hour early. Because our schools start at 9:00 and staff get there by 8:15, I am always in the office by 7:00. From 7:00 to 8:00 I am able to really focus, to read, and to write. I have two rules—no Internet and no e-mail until 8:30. Eliminating these distractions can dramatically increase your productivity first thing in the morning.

Blog First Thing in the Morning

Author and speaker Brian Tracy often shares a productivity concept called "Eat that frog. Do the most difficult thing first." (For further reference, see his book *Eat That Frog.*) School leaders I have talked to who only dream about creating a blog often blame "busyness" as their reason for not getting started. To start a blog, to build a following, and to make a larger impact on the educational world beyond your own school—you need to make blogging a priority. Writing first thing in the morning and posting your content online is a great way to start your day. By following this routine, you will have a renewed sense of accomplishment, no matter how difficult the rest of your day becomes.

Reflect in the Afternoon

Another strategy for blogging is to use your afternoon commute. Most school leaders I talk to are exhausted by the end of the day. They can't wait to get home. They spend their fifteen to thirty minutes driving home exhausted, in zombie mode, just a numb mess. Instead of this, take out your phone, use your voice recording app, and audibly process your day. Complain about that teacher who fails to hand in lesson plans. Scream about that student who has been given a third, fourth, and fifth chance and still is messing it up. Use your day for content. Of course you will change the names and situations to protect privacy, but you will also capture the content while it is still fresh. The mind is a great place for having ideas but a terrible place for keeping them. Ensure that you capture your ideas in the moment.

Tip The key to my writing this book and to your writing your blog is a little computer application called Freedom (macfreedom.com). Freedom is a simple productivity application that locks you away from the Internet on Mac or Windows computers for an amount of time you specify. I have found that fifteen minutes of Freedom, four times per day, goes a long way to increasing my productivity and getting important tasks accomplished.

FEATURES OF YOUR BLOGGING PLATFORM

Three major platforms exist for creating and hosting your blog: Blogger, Word-Press, and Tumblr. Each of these platforms offers tools for posting, editing, sharing, and distributing your content. For the sake of simplicity, this chapter will focus on my favorite blog platform, WordPress. The features that WordPress offers make it an attractive option for beginners and experts alike. These include hosting, themes, and plug-ins:

- **Hosting.** Visit the WordPress website and choose a title for your blog. Your site will appear at YourBlogTitle.wordpress.com for free. For only eight dollars per year, you could personalize your blog's URL, whereby the address would appear at YourBlogTitle.com. Title your blog something like *Learning Redesigned* or *ClassroomExpectations.com.* Your blog can be officially sanctioned through your district, or more likely it can be a personal site that allows you to express yourself in a space not formally affiliated with your school. Over the course of my education career so far, I have worked for six different educational institutions, and during that time I have always maintained my own personal blog with no issues. You are likely to change jobs several times and will not be with the same school for your entire career. Even if you are with the same district, you will probably have different administrators with different perspectives and different technology directors with different policies. I recommend that you establish your own blog that is not officially connected to any school. This will allow you to maintain all of the content and the rights to that content.

- **Themes.** A theme will allow you to change the appearance of your blog with just a few clicks. You can decide whether you want photos to be large, small, scrollable, or arranged like a photo book; what color the font and text size should be; and the format of the content.

- **Plug-ins.** Plug-ins allow different actions to be taken on your content, from automatic sharing to embedding multimedia and adding subscriber features. For a refresher on both themes and plug-ins, revisit Chapter Four concerning your school website.

BUILDING YOUR PLATFORM

All school leaders I speak with want to grow their career. They are interested in having more responsibility, making a larger impact on the educational conversation, publishing their work, moving to a warmer climate, working at a school or school district with a better reputation, earning more money, having an impact on more students, and building a legacy. All of these are reasons to blog. Once you have been blogging for a while, you will begin to find that one of the side benefits of frequently blogging is that you can grow a platform.

Your platform is defined as your level of influence over others in your field. Your thoughts and ideas can have an impact on other educational leaders, and your blog can become a go-to source that helps you share your conference presentations, your meeting highlights, and your other ideas with a larger audience. Your blog opens up new opportunities to talk to other educational leaders at a conference who have read your thoughts, tried out your ideas, and are excited to share the success. You might even get a writing contract and release your first book, sharing it with others in your community and being recognized as the thought leader that you have grown to be. The larger you grow your platform and the more people who read what you have to say and share your content, the greater the impact your experiences will have in the field of education. The more potential you have to generate side revenues through your blog, the bigger difference you can make in the long run. Here are a few specific strategies to grow your platform:

- **Use a multiposting service.** Use such tools as TubeMogul or Ping.fm to ensure that your content appears in multiple places online.

- **Join LinkedIn.** LinkedIn is a widely accepted tool for building a professional network. The WordPress plug-in on LinkedIn enables your blog posts to automatically appear on your LinkedIn profile. For more information on LinkedIn, see Chapter Thirteen.

- **Post on YouTube.** Posting regular video clips and then embedding these video clips on your blog as part of your post will help you reach a larger audience. For more information YouTube, review Chapter Six.

- **Measure your impact.** One way to measure your impact online is called the "Klout Score" from klout.com. Klout is an online service that evaluates and measures your influence over others based on several criteria, including the number of people whom you follow and who follow you on Twitter; how many blog readers, subscribers, and commenters you have; and other factors. Klout can provide additional motivation to encourage you to post frequently on your blog.

BEST PRACTICES FOR BLOGGING

Here are a few best practices to help your blog become a valuable tool for growing your professional practice and reputation:

Make It Look Professional

Using the freely available themes on WordPress, a professional looking blog can be established with little time or technical knowledge. As also noted in Chapter Four, avoid overused or outdated online elements (such as broken links and Comic Sans font) to ensure visitors view your site as one maintained by a professional. Find inspiration for the style and design of your blog from websites of reputable companies and news outlets to help ensure a professional design.

Keep It Updated

It is important to keep your blog updated. Establish a writing routine, making blogging part of your weekly schedule. By posting infrequently, you discourage readers from checking your blog for updated content. Some of the best blogs are updated every single day. Although this is not my chosen strategy, there is value in establishing readership. When you post every day, your subscribers will depend on content from you. This expectation of content builds trust and establishes rapport. As a school leader, you will always have something to write about. Following the tips for coming up with new topics given earlier in this chapter, you can find something to write about every single day. Again, keep it updated. The worst thing you can do is to post once or twice and never touch it again. People will expect you to update your content, and when you don't, they will lose interest.

Keep It Appropriate

Although your blog is a great opportunity to engage your school community in an authentic way, remember that what you say will be seen as representing your school. Be sure to avoid politics, controversial personal opinions, or anything else that might get you into hot water. Your words as a school leader have a greater impact than those of another "private citizen." The best approach for your blog is to focus on your field, sharing your perspective on matters that affect your school community and the larger educational landscape.

Make It Accessible

Make sure that your blog content is accessible. This means that people will be able to explore your content no matter what platform they are on or where they are checking from. There are a number ways to do this. The first of these is to use a platform that's mobile friendly. WordPress, Tumblr, and Blogger are all great platforms to use. Be careful not to have excessive links, ads, and sidebar content. Keeping your layout simple helps ensure that all readers will be able to engage in your content without distraction. Some education blogs are difficult to read because they are too cluttered with superfluous sidebar quotes, flashing banners, and website "badges" stating blog rankings, the number of followers, and a list of the most popular tags. Avoid all of this nonsense and focus on posting great content that provides value for the reader.

Share your blog content across multiple platforms by connecting your Word-Press blog to Facebook and Twitter or by using a multiposting service, such as Ping.fm. This ensures that every time you write a new blog post, a notification is sent to your followers on those networks. The more often your blog is sent across the Web, the more opportunities your readers have to engage in your content. Each of these posts on social media platforms links back to your blog and will help increase your blog's visibility in search engines. If your topic is "Teaching Students with Dyslexia," for example, anytime someone searches "students" and "dyslexia" your blog is likely to appear near the top of the rankings as long as you blog frequently, post on multiple platforms, and have multiple links tracking back to your blog from other sites. All of these links are an indication of your influence. The more influential you are, the more that Google, Bing, and other search engines will believe that you should be near the top of the list.

Make It Searchable

Some of the best content has never been read because no one can find it. Ensure that your blog is searchable by using accurate tags, keywords, and categories. Spend just as much time tagging your content with keywords and categorizing your posts as you do on developing the content. Help your content spread across the Web by linking back to other related blogs and resources. Ensure that the search box is visible in a primary place on your blog (usually the top right corner). Consider how others will find your content in the future; you want your content to have a long shelf life. Great content that can't be found is not valuable.

Make It Shareable

A key component of successful blogs is that they are shareable. Implement tools that make it easy to distribute and share your content. Once readers engage in your content and value what you have to say, the next step is for them to spread that content to others whom they can influence. This is how you grow your own influence and how your content reaches a larger audience. To help your blog be more shareable, install a "ShareThis" button on your blog. This tool is easily installed on a WordPress blog and allows readers to click just one button to spread the content to their social networks.

ONGOING SOCIAL ENGAGEMENT WITH A SCHOOL LEADER'S BLOG

A school leader's blog can help build ongoing social engagement online (see Figure 11.3). From building awareness, to inviting feedback and collaboration, to drawing attention to important topics, a blog is your platform for sharing your voice online.

Awareness

A school leader's blog is a great tool for building awareness, as there is no limit to the number of posts, the length of the content, or the subject matter covered. This blog can be a great platform for sharing both detailed explanations of decisions made at the school level and ideas about school leadership with a larger online audience beyond the local school community.

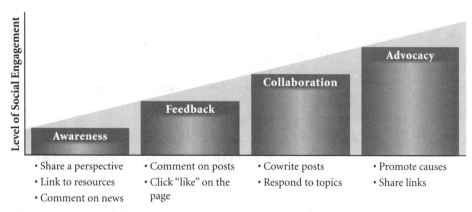

Figure 11.3 Social Engagement with a School Leader's Blog

Feedback

A school leader's blog is also a great place for receiving feedback. Posting articles on your blog can lead you to obtain feedback through commenting, through receiving likes on social networks, and through having a website visitor e-mail you to give you direct feedback.

Collaboration

Many bloggers use the sharing features of blogs to write collaborative posts. These can take the form of an interview conversation with e-mails back and forth or a text transcription of a Skype conversation. A collaborative post can share the ideas of both writers, help them improve the quality of their ideas, and build their respective followings.

Advocacy

Use your blog to promote causes that are important to you. Invite blog readers to give to DonorsChoose.org or other worthy organizations. Ask blog readers to enter the e-mail addresses of others who might be interested in subscribing to your blog. Reach out to those new contacts with a simple e-mail.

COMMON SCHOOL TASKS BEFORE AND AFTER STARTING A BLOG

Maintaining a blog can change the way you complete common school tasks, such as making announcements and sharing best practices.

Task or Goal	Traditional Method	Using Your Blog
Making announcements	Traditionally, school leaders would make announcements in two ways. First, they would make the announcement over the intercom, interrupting the happenings in the classroom. Second, they would stand up at an assembly and make an audible announcement, trying to get the attention of all of the students. Students who were not in attendance or who were not paying attention would miss the announcement because it was only made once.	Announcements made on your blog can be written or recorded, edited for content, posted at your convenience, and scheduled to appear at a specific time. Students and parents alike can visit your blog whenever they want, as many times as they want, to read the announcement. They can even give their feedback by commenting or "liking" the posts.
Sharing best practices	School leaders would share best practices by creating a PowerPoint presentation to give at a conference. They would physically travel to the conference and speak to the audience in attendance. Those who are not in attendance would miss the presentation. To share best practices with faculty, a faculty meeting would be held on the school campus. The school leader would encourage faculty to keep working hard and doing a good job.	School leaders can upload the text of any presentation to their blog. They can even include a video archive of a live presentation, which is accessible by anyone at any time and is also keyword searchable. You can share best practices with faculty on your blog by including links, a video to watch, and other multimedia along with your original thoughts. This can be scheduled to appear on your blog at any time, and you can send a link to the blog post to your faculty. One of the added benefits of this method is that other teachers and school administrators not at your school will also be encouraged through this content, which has been posted publicly for anyone to access.

GETTING STARTED WITH YOUR BLOG

Question for Reflection: If you could share only three pieces of advice with someone entering the teaching profession, what would you say to that person? You now have your first blog topic.

First Steps

1. Brainstorm potential topics about which you would like to blog.

2. Examine your bookshelf. Google the names of two or three authors you admire to locate their blog. Discover how they are using online tools to engage their audience.

3. Visit the website of your local newspaper. Create a user account and comment on a news story relevant to your school community.

Mobile Devices

Innovative school leaders use mobile devices to have authentic, ongoing conversations with their school community. Embracing your cell phone as a tool to communicate with your parent community can help you become a more engaged school leader. Topics covered in this chapter include

- More than a phone
- Introduction to apps
- Increasing your productivity with mobile devices
- Cell phones and parents
- Cell phones and students
- Ongoing social engagement with mobile devices

- Another new category of mobile devices
- Getting started with mobile devices

MORE THAN A PHONE

Mobile devices have dramatically changed over the past few years, increasing in both capacity and capability. The mobile device in your pocket is now more powerful than the laptop you may have had just a few years ago. The most dramatic improvement has been in the speed of information transfer, as cell phones are now able to stream and even download large amounts of data. With mobile devices, we are now able to watch live television from our iPhone at the airport, or to have a live Skype videoconference in an elevator. Wireless connectivity, now enabled through mobile devices, has profoundly shifted the way we are able to communicate. We were once required to sit in our office checking e-mail or typing a document; now we can create from any place we happen to be. People are now accessible 24/7, wherever they are, and this reality has only served to increase the expectations of accessibility and engagement from parent communities.

The device in your pocket is more than a telephone. It is a camera, a mobile library, a video player, and a communication device, enabling you to make phone calls, send text messages and e-mails, and have real-time video conversations with anyone in the world. This chapter includes many of the mobile devices and applications that have been recently developed, from smartphones (including iPhone, Android, and Blackberry devices) to tablets (including the iPad, Kindle, Nook, and others). Although the educational applications of these technology advances are continually being explored, this chapter aims to share proven strategies you can use to better take advantage of mobile technologies today. The theories shared apply to all of these platforms, even if the specific apps have different names.

After introducing you to mobile devices in general and apps in particular, this chapter focuses specifically on how to use mobile devices in your school leadership practice. We'll start with improving your own personal productivity because saving time and being better organized can dramatically improve your educational leadership. After that, we'll investigate the current state of cell phones and students, looking, hopefully with fresh eyes, at the ban that most schools have implemented on mobile devices in the hands of students on campus. We'll also consider ways to use these mobile devices to increase student learning, enhance student engagement, and make an impact on student achievement. After that, we'll conclude by applying the ongoing social engagement model to mobile technology, discovering new ways to build awareness, enhance feedback, increase collaboration, and empower your community to advocate for your school.

Available Tools

Mobile devices, from cell phones to tablet computers, are now at their lowest price point ever. Smartphones, including the iPhone, can start for as little as $99, and tablet computers, including the Nook, Kindle, and iPad, start as low as $199. These price points are getting into the realm of the cost of just a few textbooks, making them an obvious choice for today's school leaders. Through the open-source Android operating system or the iOS iPhone system, using apps and the Web on mobile devices is easier than ever.

Setting Up Your Devices

Smartphones make it easy to transfer your data from one phone to another. Starting with your current phone, every time you upgrade you simply transfer your information. Most cell phone providers also offer a free transfer service, enabling you to quickly and easily take your contacts with you to the new phone.

INTRODUCTION TO APPS

Applications are the key technology that has transformed mobile devices from traditional phones into powerful mobile computing machines. Apps are small programs designed for a specific purpose. These mobile applications are written by programmers in diverse industries, with diverse intentions. The barrier to entering software development to create these mobile applications is very low. What once required a master's degree in computer science and an entire team of engineers can now be designed by a high school student on his or her laptop. This means that applications are becoming more individualized and personalized. Apps exist that allow you to create a multimedia slide show presentation, to manage your finances and trade stocks, to consult an attorney, to track your physical fitness levels, to measure your food intake, and to manage your diabetes. For the sake of simplicity I have chosen to focus on the Apple iPhone device, although the Android operating system features phones and apps capable of many of the same functions. With over five hundred thousand apps available in the Apple App Store, there is truly an app for everything.

Downloading Apps

To download an app on your iPhone, simply create an iTunes account. Your username, which is your e-mail, and your password must be associated with a credit card to use the store. Whenever you want to download an app, you simply click "download" and enter your password. If there is a fee for the app, your credit card is automatically charged. Most developers have created a free version and a paid version of their apps. If you are wary of purchasing a new app but want to try it out, download the free version. If you are finding value, then pay the extra dollar or two to download the full app. Most free apps will have limited features and functionality, and the paid version can make a dramatic improvement in regard to the capability of that app. The best way to learn about apps is by looking online for reviews, both on blogs and in the App Store, where people commonly post ratings and reviews. Read the ratings and look at the reviews to help decide if an app will work for you. For those of you just starting to use an iPhone for the first time, I would recommend a budget of $10 to $20 a month to download and try out different apps. If $1.99 can save you twenty minutes every day, isn't it worth buying the app?

Adopting New Apps

One of the keys to effectively using a new app on your mobile device is to do so daily. Once you have downloaded an app, commit to trying to use the app every day for a week. After trying the app for seven days in a row, if you are not satisfied with the app, then delete it. There is no need to use it again. This will help prevent "app overload," whereby your phone is full of apps you never use. A number of the apps that I regularly use took time to learn and adapt to, but now I can't live without some of them.

INCREASING YOUR PRODUCTIVITY WITH MOBILE DEVICES

Saving time, being better organized, and more efficiently communicating with your team can dramatically improve your educational leadership. No matter which mobile devices you use, there are numerous apps to assist you in the management of your school. Technology can make you more organized, productive, and efficient, but the information overload and constant interruption can also detract from any productivity gain. Successful school leaders find ways to manage the noise, to clear the clutter, and to focus on what's important.

The following subsections outline several key ways to increase your productivity dramatically using the available apps on your phone or tablet. Although this chapter focuses on the iPhone, which I personally believe is the best mobile platform available today, many of the theories and even the applications still apply, particularly if you are using an Android device. We will look at seven ways mobile devices can be used to increase your productivity, starting with to-do apps, moving to calendar and appointment management, then messaging and communication, custom mobile apps, document access and backup, professional development, and finally personal health.

To-Do Apps

Your mobile device can serve as an always-with-you to-do list, ensuring that you capture and manage specific key tasks. Apps abound for managing your to-do list, some great, some terrible. In just one day, you will see a radical difference in your workday if you use your phone to manage your to-do list. All day long you will be reminded of small tasks that you need to accomplish, from sending a document to a teacher to returning a phone call to a parent or checking in on a student. There is no way that your brain can hold all of those tasks in an efficient way.

My favorite app for managing my to-do lists, simply titled Reminders, comes built in with the iOS system on your iPhone. Reminders is backed up on your computer, so you never lose your to-do list. It also has time-based and location-based reminders, as well as the option for context-based lists. Figure 12.1 demonstrates how you can use the Reminders app to (1) select your context-based list, (2) set a reminder for the to-do item, and (3) add details to the reminder.

- **Time-based reminders.** When you add a new to-do item, you can have your phone notify you when you are to complete that task. For example, if you need to call someone at a specific time, set a to-do item in Reminders. Let's say you need to call Julie at 4:30 p.m. At 4:30 sharp your phone will beep in your pocket, and the text on the screen will remind you to call Julie.

Figure 12.1 Screenshot: Reminders App

- **Location-based reminders.** This feature is even better than time-based reminders, because you are reminded to complete a task based on your phone's GPS. You can choose to be notified of a to-do item when you arrive at or leave a certain location. Before Reminders, I frequently forgot to pick up my dry cleaning. Now every time I drive near my dry cleaner a reminder pops up on my phone reminding me to pick up the dry cleaning. This has saved me a lot of time and helps ensure that I always have pressed shirts. You can use Reminders to tell you not to forget something when you are leaving a specific location, or to remind you to complete a task as soon as you arrive at school. Reminders can access the addresses in your contact list. To create a new location-based reminder, simply add a contact for that location.

- **Context-based lists.** To help manage the number of items on my to-do list, I use context-based lists. A context-based list is a list of items to do that are categorized by a specific location or activity. My context-based lists include @e-mail, @phone, @school, @errands, and @meeting. When an item comes up, either through e-mail, in person, on the phone, or in my mind, I simply open my to-do app and enter that task into the appropriate context-based list, fully trusting that it will be there when I need it.

Calendar and Appointment Management

A built-in feature of most smartphones is the ability to manage your calendar. Although this may be a basic feature, it is one of the most powerful on your phone. I am still surprised when I talk to school leaders who don't manage their calendar from their phone. When you don't plan your day, you spend all day putting out fires as they happen rather than strategically accomplishing important tasks. The Calendar app on your iPhone can help you take back control of your daily schedule. Features of the Calendar app include the following:

> Author and efficiency expert Tim Ferriss writes, "What you do is infinitely more important than how you do it. Efficiency is still important, but it is useless unless applied to the right things."
>
> Tim Ferriss, *The Four Hour Work Week* (New York: Crown, 2009), 70.

- **Day planning.** You can see your plan for the day, and using the agenda view on the Calendar app you can look at your day in a new way. Your device gives you multiple views of your appointments, responsibilities, and interactions with others.

- **Meeting invitations.** Send out and receive meeting invitations on your phone using the Calendar app. Include other people as attendees to a calendar event, and track who is attending the meeting, ensuring that these people have received the invitation and responded appropriately. Once they have responded, the notification of that meeting will appear for them.

- **Reminders.** The Calendar app has a reminder function as well that can play a ringtone of your choice a certain number of minutes before your meeting.

- **Calendar syncing.** Every appointment that you set on your calendar, whether through Google Calendar, iCal, or the Calendar app on your phone, can include an attachment, notes, reminders, and other participants. All of these data are shared between multiple systems, ensuring that you always have current information. These data are also automatically backed up, both on the Google Calendar server and on your computer. Losing your mobile device doesn't mean losing your data; you just need to sync your new device with your Apple or Gmail username and password. The data "cloud" ensures that you never lose your important information again.

- **Availability sharing.** Managing your calendar and sharing it with key staff members can dramatically improve your productivity. Not only can you share your calendar with others but also you can view their calendar on your phone. Having access to your team's availability helps with scheduling meetings and appointments.

- **Appointment notes.** You can make additional comments in the note section of your calendar dedicated to a specific appointment. For example, you might add the call-in number of your appointment for a conference call. When the appointment comes, you simply check the notes and dial the number. No more searching through old e-mails. While you are working throughout the day, if you remember something to ask at the meeting, simply open your calendar, find that upcoming appointment, and add to the notes of that appointment. When entering a meeting, make it a regular habit to look at the notes you have left for yourself on your phone for that meeting. This will help ensure that you never forget a question or a reminder to a colleague.

Justin Baeder, principal of Olympic View Elementary School in Seattle, writes about how he uses mobile devices to manage teacher observations. "Whenever I can get into classrooms, I visit the room at the top of my list (in OmniFocus), take notes in Evernote, email them to the teacher, and move the teacher's name to the bottom of my list in OmniFocus."

"Using the iPad for Paperless Walkthroughs," posted October 21, 2010, http://blogs.edweek.org/edweek/LeaderTalk/2010/10/using_the_ipad_for_paperless_w.html.

- **Agenda attachments.** You can even attach a document to a calendar item. For example, you can attach the agenda to a meeting appointment on your calendar. This means that you just need to take your phone to the meeting, and the agenda is easy to access.

Tip Using my alarm app, I have four alarms scheduled for when I typically have downtime—after students are in class, before and after lunch, and right before the end of the day. The alarm is labeled, "Am I working on something of value or just avoiding the important?" This prevents me from getting stuck checking e-mail and helps me focus on completing important tasks during the day so I can leave the office at a decent hour.

Messaging and Communication

There are many apps that help you better communicate through your mobile device. This subsection looks at four applications on your mobile device to improve your messaging and communication, including iMessage, e-mail, Away-Find, and Dragon Dictation.

- **iMessage.** There are many apps that allow for text and picture messaging. With text messaging rates now lower than ever, using the built in iMessage app works for most mobile device users. Most smartphones now enable you to send a text message to more than one recipient at a time. Build a list of all of the teachers' cell phone numbers on your phone, and copy this list into the text or notepad feature of your phone. Save it as "faculty contact list." When you need to send a quick text to your teachers, for example, "We will be meeting fifteen minutes later," or "The buses have been delayed," you can simply access this notepad document, copy the phone numbers, paste them into the text message, and send the message to all of your teachers at the same time. Using group texting ensures that teachers get the message immediately. Most teachers have their phone on them at all times, whether in their pocket or in their purse. The phone notifies them, through vibration or a ringtone, that they have a new message. This prevents such class interruptions as announcements over the school's intercom or the school leader knocking on the classroom door.

- **E-mail.** Your phone's built in e-mail system is one of the most powerful features of this mobile device. Although it is a scaled-down version of a more comprehensive e-mail system, such as Mail from Apple or Microsoft Outlook, it can still dramatically improve your communication. An e-mail app on your mobile device lets you send an e-mail from wherever you are, and lets you check e-mails as they come in. Be careful, however, not to use e-mail as an instant messaging service—many e-mail programs only sync every five minutes.

- **AwayFind.** If you do find yourself checking your e-mail every five minutes, you might want to download AwayFind. This "e-mail alert notification app" helps you get away from your inbox by sending you a text message or voice call on your mobile phone when you receive an e-mail you've been waiting for. You can set up the parameters to look for specific subjects or senders, ensuring that you immediately receive a notification if an important message you've been expecting arrives in your e-mail inbox. AwayFind even has a great feature that notifies you of a new message from someone you're meeting with that day. This one feature alone has prevented me from attending meetings that were cancelled at the last minute.

- **Dragon Dictation.** This voice transcription app is one of my most frequently used apps. You simply open the Dragon Dictation app and click the red button to record. Then you say whatever is on your mind, whether it is a reminder, a short message, or a status update. It records you and transcribes your voice recording into text. You can then share this content in a number of ways: as a Facebook or Twitter update, as a text message or e-mail, or as a copy to your clipboard for pasting into a word processing program. This can be very powerful in enabling you to text while you are driving without using your hands, or to send a quick message while walking. This technology will only get smarter, allowing you to use your phone to message people through the power of voice commands.

Custom Mobile Apps

Many websites and computer software programs now have their own custom mobile applications. Usually these mobile applications are scaled-down versions of the full website or program, allowing you access to only the most frequently used features. Following are a few examples of custom apps we use at our school:

- **Constant Contact.** Most eNewsletter services have their own mobile application to help you manage your eNewsletter campaigns. The Constant Contact app has such features as tracking opens and clicks, creating a new campaign, and accessing contact information on the go. This app doesn't have all of the features of the full website, but it is very convenient for quickly checking your eNewsletter statistics.

- **Facebook.** All smartphones now have a Facebook app that allows you to update your school's Facebook page on the go. I frequently update our school's Facebook page with pictures of school activities while making my daily rounds. Here's how:

1. Open the Facebook app, and search for your school's page.

2. Click "take photo."

3. Upload the photo and add a description.

4. Review your updated page.

- **WordPress.** The free WordPress mobile app lets you update and create new posts and pages for your WordPress blog or website. You can update your school website or your school leader's blog from anywhere you have your mobile device.

Document Access and Backup

One challenge school leaders face is managing the continual collection of paper documents. We often attend meetings, complete observations, and make presentations in which we are required to have a specific piece of paper with us. Without that piece of paper, we won't have the right statistic, the quote, or the data we need. Paper is finite and is no longer a great way to manage information.

- What if you lose the paper?
- What if you leave the paper in your briefcase or office?
- What if you lend the paper to someone else?

Imagine never misplacing a document again. Using your mobile device, you can have a reliable system for keeping and organizing documents.

- **Evernote.** Several apps exist for backing up your documents to an online server, often referred to as "the cloud." My favorite is Evernote because it enables you to quickly back up all of your files. This is powerful. The entire text of all documents in Evernote is searchable, so even if you quickly titled a document "volunteer list," you can find it by searching for the exact name of the event. Evernote also doubles as a note-taking app. When you write a note on your phone using Evernote, the note is automatically synced to the cloud. Evernote also allows you to post multimedia, such as video, audio, and pictures, which are all searchable. All of these cloud-based solutions store your documents on a secure, password-protected server. Evernote is the first application that allows you to sync every document to the cloud with optical character recognition. Even photocopied or scanned documents are searchable from the Evernote app on your phone, your iPad, or your laptop, or from the Evernote website. Evernote automatically uses optical character recognition, or OCR, to convert scanned documents to searchable text.

- **Mobile Receipt.** As a school leader, managing your school finances, particularly purchases, invoices, and receipts, can be a challenge. It is estimated that the average manager spends six to eight hours per month managing expense reports. Allow your mobile phone to make this process much easier. One app to try is called Mobile Receipt. Every time you make a purchase, simply open up Mobile Receipt and take a picture of the receipt. You then have several options to categorize and make notes on the purchase. As a backup I also write on the back of the receipt exactly what the purchase was and the category as a backup. All of this information is saved on your Mobile Receipt account and is easily attachable to your expense reports. Mobile Receipt recognizes the text on the receipt and puts the data into a spreadsheet, helping you complete your expense reports with ease.

Professional Development

The device in your pocket or in your briefcase can help you improve your professional practice. Your phone allows you to have a connected learning lab with you at all times. You can download podcasts on iTunes, audiobooks with the Audible app, and e-books with the Kindle or iBooks app. All of these options allow you to learn on the go, improving your professional practice. Many of these apps also have social features, allowing you to share great resources with your faculty team directly from your mobile device.

Personal Health

Most school leaders wake up between 4:30 and 5:30 in the morning to get ready for a school day that starts at 7:00. Waking up groggy and tired is something that every school leader struggles with; and often educators welcome any advice for better waking and managing sleep. Well, there is an app for that! SleepCycle is a smart alarm clock that measures your movement throughout the night. You simply set the alarm on the app, plug the phone into a power source, and leave the phone next to your pillow overnight. There is a correlation between your movement and your state of consciousness. Most alarm clocks are set for a specific time. People who wake up at 5:15 every day find that on one day they're wide awake at 5:15 and on another day they're very groggy. Without getting too far into the science, the basic reason for this is that on days that you feel awake, the 5:15 is at the end of your thirty-minute sleep cycle. The days that you are feeling groggy, you are being awoken in the middle of your sleep cycle, out of deep sleep. This app measures your sleep cycle and intelligently wakes you up when you are most awake. Simply choose a thirty-minute window during which to wake up, with the absolutely latest time as the highest number. For example, if you traditionally wake up at 5:15 but don't mind waking up at 5:30, set the alarm for 5:00 to 5:30. SleepCycle will measure your movement and wake you up at the optimal time during that thirty-minute window. One day you will wake up at 5:25, and one day you will wake up at 5:03. I have used SleepCycle for over a year, and I always wake up energized and refreshed. Often I open my eyes, look around, wonder, *What time is it?*—and that's when the alarm goes off. SleepCycle knows when I am awake (based on movement) and intelligently wakes me up. Waking up rested and ready for your day can make a dramatic impact on your outlook. Your attitude and behavior toward colleagues will set the tone for your school. This one app alone could completely change the attitude and behavior of your entire faculty. When you are positive and alert, you inspire others to be the same.

CELL PHONES AND PARENTS

Often in the life of a school leader, direct communication with your parent community is the only solution to a difficult situation. Your cell phone can be an effective tool for engaging parents when you follow these proven strategies.

Your Cell Phone Number

Whether you have a school-issued cell phone (preferred) or a personal cell phone, your cell phone is now an essential tool to communicate with your school parents on the go. You can use your cell phone for making and receiving calls and for sending and receiving text messages.

- **Calls.** Consider giving out your cell phone number. Numbers you don't recognize can be sent to voicemail. By allowing families to leave messages on your cell phone, you'll be able to hear directly from your constituents. You can enter their information in your phone in case you need to contact them in the future. On my e-mail signature and business card, I have my cell phone number. I believe that I work for my students and their families. It is therefore important that they be able to contact me directly when necessary. Families understand that this is my personal cell phone number and are reluctant to call it unless it is absolutely necessary. On average, I only get a few phone calls on that phone per day, most of which I would need to handle anyway. Because I have given out my personal cell phone number, families feel like they have a voice and a personal connection to the school leader.

- **Text messaging.** The cell phone is no longer just for voice communication— it's also for text messaging, photo sharing, and now even video transfer. When dealing with student issues, I prefer to call parents on their cell phone. After the conversation, I send a quick thank you text and add the parent to my contacts. I'll probably need this number in the future. Parents may not answer their phone while at work, but they may be able to read a text. There are even systems available now that allow you to send a mass text message to all cell phones in your parent contact database.

Voicemail Hotline

If giving out your cell phone number makes you nervous, consider setting up a voicemail hotline. A voicemail hotline allows you to hear directly from the people whom you serve and helps you receive the direct feedback you need to continually improve your school. There are several advantages of establishing a voicemail hotline rather than having a traditional voicemail extension:

- **Calls never ring to an actual phone.** Families can leave messages at any time without worrying about someone answering the phone.

- **Messages are e-mailed to you.** There's no need to log on to a website or be at your computer to check your messages. They are automatically sent to you.

- **It records the sender's phone number.** Phone numbers are captured for responding to the sender.

- **It is cost effective.** Establishing a voicemail hotline is far cheaper than setting up another cell phone to handle parent phone calls to a school number.

Two options for setting up your own voicemail hotline are Skype and K7. Skype is a Web-based alternative to a traditional telephone. K7 is a free service that allows you to set up an inbound voicemail hotline. Both options forward your voicemail messages to your e-mail inbox, allowing you to listen to the messages at your computer or on your smartphone.

- **Skype.** Skype's Online Number service allows you to create a local phone number with online voicemail for less than ten dollars a month.
- **K7.** This is a free alternative to Skype's online voicemail. You can sign up for a telephone number with a Seattle area code. When families call your number, your custom greeting plays, and they can leave you a message.

Either one of these options gives families the feeling that they are being listened to. A voicemail hotline also allows you to have much more authentic conversations with them and eliminates some of the gatekeepers preventing you from truly knowing the cares and concerns of your students and parents. This allows you to be in tune with your school community.

Emergencies

Mobile devices can be instrumental in ensuring efficient communication directly with your parents and student community in the case of any emergencies at your school, from a minor bus accident or delayed field trip bus to a dramatic incident, such as a fire or hostage situation. Given the rapid pace of the development of mobile technology, revisit your school's emergency management plan, and consider ways to use text messaging and voice communication to keep your school informed in an emergency. Mobile devices may help you do any of the following:

- **Text back.** One tool is called TextMarks, which allows your community to send a text to a specific number, with a specific code, and receive a text message back. This can be set up to dynamically feed news or the latest information when someone sends a text. We've used it for student recruitment in the past: "Text 'students' to 41411 to receive information about enrolling in this school." But the same could be true for school cancellations: "Text 'school' to 41411 to receive updated information about school cancellations." Because the message is updated from a website, you can access and modify it from anywhere.

Having the text-back feature might be your best strategy for communicating with your parents, particularly those who do not have Internet access or who primarily use their phone.

- **Send a text blast.** Everyone on your text message list can receive an announcement or update. One way to enable this is Call-Em-All. Call-Em-All allows you to send a short message using text messaging to everyone in your entire group at one time. The rates are fairly reasonable, especially for one-time use, and the message can be scheduled to be sent out immediately. Call-Em-All also has a voice broadcast feature, which can send an audio recording out to all of the phone numbers you have on file. We have used this for reminders for report card nights, open houses, and enrollment information. However, it could also be used for school cancellations and other emergencies.

- **Broadcast your message across networks.** When you have an urgent announcement to send out to your community, you want to use as many networks as possible to ensure that everybody has received that information in a timely way. Using a multiposting service, such as Ping.fm, is an easy way to do this. Some families will check your website, some will log on to Facebook, and others will expect an update on Twitter. Posting to these networks in addition to text messaging will help ensure that your school community is aware of the latest information.

CELL PHONES AND STUDENTS

Most schools I work with currently have an outright ban on student cell phones in the classroom, if not a campuswide ban. The most common cell phone rule I've seen is, "The first time a student is seen with a cell phone, he or she receives a warning; the second time, the cell phone is taken away for a day; and the third time, it is taken away for the rest of the semester. A parent is required to come to the school to pick up the phone." The rationale for these rules is understandable. With so many horror stories concerning the ways students have used cell phones, it is understandable why schools have banned cell phones completely from campus.

There are, however, schools across the country that have adopted a tamer approach to managing cell phones. This might include allowing cell phones in common areas or outside of class, or establishing a courtesy policy whereby cell phones are allowed to be used at any time. In other words, there are schools that are looking at cell phones in a different way.

While acknowledging that challenges do exist when students bring cell phones to school, it cannot be ignored that cell phones are a necessary tool in today's world. Students will be using cell phones to conduct business, communicate with others, and improve their productivity both in college and in the workplace. As the role of K–12 education is to prepare students for college and a career, the rationale is clear for why it would be foolish for all student cell phones to be completely banned. There must be appropriate ways, or appropriate times, for cell phones to be used.

Here are a few ideas to help train students to use mobile devices effectively, like adults do in the real world:

- **Note-taking apps.** Today's mobile devices have note-taking apps available to help students better digest the classroom content. From a simple notepad app to handwriting recognition apps and apps specifically designed for students, there are some very effective options that can help students take notes in class, remember main points, demonstrate their learning, and better prepare for assessments.

- **To-do apps.** To-do apps can help students better manage their time and remember which homework assignments to do. Students can even set alerts and reminders to study a certain chapter, to complete a particular reading, or to prepare for a test.

- **E-mail.** As explained many times in this book, e-mail is a necessary communication tool in today's world. Students can use e-mail to ask questions of the teacher, to forward assignments or questions to each other, and to reach out to experts in the community.

> In their wonderful book Teaching Generation Text, *authors Lisa Nielsen and Willyn Webb challenge educators to think "beyond the ban" on cell phones in schools. They explain, "Today's phones can alert students to study; serve as a smart vehicle to take notes; provide instant, on-demand answers and research; and even provide a great way to record and capture student oral reports or responses to polls and quizzes."*
>
> Lisa Nielsen and Willyn Webb, *Teaching Generation Text: Using Cell Phones to Enhance Learning* (San Francisco, Jossey-Bass, 2011), 1.

- **Mobile polls.** Poll Everywhere is a system that allows students to respond to teachers' questions in real time through the use of mobile polling, similar to the student response system clickers available. When students have their phone in the class with them, they are able to use it for mobile polling: checking in on assignments, responding to teacher questions, and even taking quizzes.

- **Portfolio updates.** As Chapter Ten on online student portfolios describes, students can effectively use WordPress or Google Sites in the classroom. They are able to update their portfolio directly from their mobile device. It can be a great use of time after they have completed an in-class assignment, for example, to conveniently post the latest information online.

ONGOING SOCIAL ENGAGEMENT WITH MOBILE DEVICES

Cell phones and mobile devices can help build ongoing social engagement online (see Figure 12.2).

Awareness

You can use mobile devices to build awareness by updating your blog, responding to e-mail, using group messaging, and posting on Twitter—among other possibilities. All of these activities will help you get news and information out to your community.

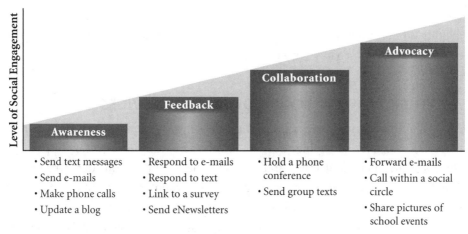

Figure 12.2 Social Engagement with Mobile Devices

Feedback

You can use your mobile device to give and receive feedback, for example by sending and receiving e-mail, making a traditional phone call, using videoconferencing (such as through FaceTime or Skype), sending out a link to a survey, or sending a text message.

Collaboration

Having a group phone call is now easier than ever. Using the iPhone, you simply add a new call when you are already connected to someone. You can quickly have three people talking to each other at the same time, collaborating on a problem and finding a solution.

Advocacy

Others can use their phones to advocate for your school. By updating their own blog, sharing a picture of what they are seeing at a parent open house online,

> *"We know that increasing parental involvement in a child's education is the single best predictor of student success,"* explains Steven Lowder, Superintendent at Hemet Unified School District. He recommends *"mobile apps that make it easy to communicate with the parents and help promote learning for the kids."*
>
> "ParentLink Adds Grades and Attendance to its K–12 Mobile Apps," accessed April 23, 2012, http://prn.to/mobile_apps _communication.

posting information from a community presentation, forwarding an e-mail, or making a phone call, visitors to your school can easily use mobile devices to get positive attention for your school.

ANOTHER NEW CATEGORY OF MOBILE DEVICES

Although this chapter has focused on such mobile devices as smartphones, there is a category of mobile devices that is beginning to have an impact on education in interesting ways, and that you may want to consider: smartpens. The Livescribe Echo pen, for example, is a computer built into a ballpoint pen. Slimmer and more powerful than its many predecessors, this smartpen uses infrared technology to read and record what you write by hand. Here is what you do:

1. **Write on Livescribe paper.** This comes in the form of spiral notebooks, Moleskine-like journals, and loose-leaf paper. This paper is printed with microscopic dots, establishing a pattern that the pen recognizes.

2. **Turn the smartpen on and start recording.** The Livescribe pen has a built-in microphone that records all of the audio it "hears" while you are writing. You take notes with the pen on the paper, and those notes are matched up or synced with the audio that is being heard at the same time.

3. **Review your notes.** Once you've recorded your notes, double-tap the pen on the paper, and the audio that was recorded when you wrote those notes will automatically play out loud. There are even advanced applications for transcribing your audio and handwritten notes to computer-based text, allowing you to use a word processing program to edit your notes for sharing and publication.

4. **Sync your Livescribe pen to your computer.** This saves a digital backup of all of your notes, both the mp3 audio and the handwritten text in pdf format.

Finally, Livescribe has built-in social sharing features that allow you to post your notes to Facebook and even to YouTube. Math teachers have found "pencasting" to be a powerful way to create Math tutorial videos for students to watch at their convenience.

GETTING STARTED WITH MOBILE DEVICES

Question for Reflection: What is your school's rule about students' using mobile devices?

First Steps

1. Meet with teachers and student representatives to discuss a BYOD (Bring Your Own Device) Day, whereby students are able to use their cell phone in a courteous way throughout the day.

2. Leave your cell phone in your car for an entire school day. This will help you understand why students struggle to leave their cell phone "off and away all day," as so many schools require.

CHAPTER 13

LinkedIn

This chapter explores LinkedIn, the premier social media tool for professional networking. You will learn specific strategies to engage your professional connections, benefiting your school's reputation as well as your future career prospects. Topics covered in this chapter include

- What is LinkedIn?
- How LinkedIn works
- Features of LinkedIn
- Ongoing social engagement with LinkedIn
- Hiring great teachers before and after LinkedIn
- LinkedIn best practices
- Next-level LinkedIn
- Getting started with LinkedIn

WHAT IS LINKEDIN?

LinkedIn is a social website focused on professional networking. It is similar to Facebook in that users create their own profile and connect to people they know. Where it differs is that Facebook connects you to your friends and family, whereas LinkedIn is for staying in touch with and growing your professional network.

Think of LinkedIn as an ever-changing online résumé. By hosting links to former and current colleagues, multimedia presentations, recommendations, and job opportunities, LinkedIn is an amazing job search tool. But it is not just about finding a new job. LinkedIn is the perfect tool for engaging a professional community of like-minded leaders, educators, and community advocates. The ease of building and accessing this professional network makes LinkedIn a school leader's most dynamic social media tool.

HOW LINKEDIN WORKS

LinkedIn is a professional networking site that allows you engage with others in your field. You first create your online portfolio on LinkedIn, adding your professional experience, education, skills, and interests. Next you reach out to people whom you know in your field. Once you've connected to these people, you can engage your network by asking questions, sharing content, and making introductions.

1. **Creating your profile.** The first step to using LinkedIn is creating your own profile. Your profile consists of your personal information, including basic profile data, job positions, education information, website links, and ways to contact you.

2. **Adding and managing connections.** LinkedIn makes it easy to add new connections by integrating with your e-mail program, such as Gmail, Hotmail, or Microsoft Outlook. You can upload your e-mail contacts and invite them to connect with you on LinkedIn.

3. **Engaging your network.** Once you are set up on LinkedIn, make it a regular part of your professional practice to communicate with and engage your network. You can engage your network by

   • *Asking questions.* By asking for help or recommendations, you give your network a reason to respond.

- *Sharing content.* Provide value to your connections on LinkedIn by sharing interesting articles, quotes, and ideas with them.

- *Making introductions.* Help the people in your network grow their own connections by introducing colleagues to each other.

> Consider whether or not you will invite fellow faculty members to connect with you on LinkedIn. Some school leaders prefer a networking strategy that does not include current faculty for fear that they will be seen as marketing themselves or looking for another job. I do recommend connecting with your team members on LinkedIn, but also caution against friending your faculty on Facebook—a tool better suited for informal, personal interaction.

FEATURES OF LINKEDIN

There is a constantly growing list of features that help improve the usability and power of LinkedIn. See Figure 13.1 for a screenshot of LinkedIn. Three great features currently available are "people you may know," groups, and profile applications.

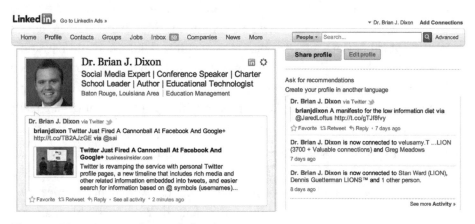

Figure 13.1 Screenshot: LinkedIn

"People You May Know"

LinkedIn is continually updating its recommendations for people whom you may know. This automated feature helps ensure that your network is constantly growing. When people you know sign up for LinkedIn, you'll receive notifications to connect with them.

Groups

You can join collegial conversations on LinkedIn and can, in a private way, communicate with groups of educators facing issues similar to your own. Many of these groups require approval by the group moderator. Discussing issues you are confronting at your school with online colleagues gives you a broader perspective and provides a network of support for handling difficult situations.

Profile Applications

LinkedIn has many applications you can choose from to further customize your LinkedIn presence. These applications help your profile move from a static online résumé to an interactive multimedia portfolio of your best work. There are applications for sharing presentations and videos, recent blog posts, and even your reading list.

- **Presentations and videos.** Both Slideshare and Google Docs allow you to share PowerPoint-like presentations on your profile with visitors. Slideshare allows you to see the number of views, has a full-screen mode, and enables users to comment on each other's presentations. Slideshare's full site allows you to upload PowerPoint presentations, customize slides, and add narration. The Google Docs application goes one step further, allowing you to embed YouTube videos into your presentations. This is currently one of the only ways to add video to your LinkedIn profile, which can help your profile really stand out.

- **Recent blog posts.** WordPress is one of the world's most popular blog platforms. WordPress provides an application that lets you link your most recent blog posts to your LinkedIn profile. Your posts will automatically appear on your LinkedIn profile when you upload content to WordPress. This is an easy way to keep your connections updated on your written content.

- **Reading list.** Add books to your LinkedIn bookshelf with Amazon's Reading List application. You can share your favorite books, link to publications you have produced, and recommend training materials in which your connections may be interested. You can also post reviews of favorite books that will be seen by other LinkedIn users, helping increase your exposure to colleagues and future connections on the site.

ONGOING SOCIAL ENGAGEMENT WITH LINKEDIN

LinkedIn is a valuable tool for increasing your ongoing social engagement in your professional practice (see Figure 13.2). This section focuses on methods and strategies for building awareness, receiving feedback, collaborating with other professionals, and empowering your connections to advocate for your school. In contrast to many of the tools discussed in this book that focus on communication from the school to the school community, LinkedIn is a great tool for one-to-one interaction between the school leader and other professional colleagues.

Awareness

There are several ways to use LinkedIn to build awareness about your school across your professional connections:

- **Share an update.** Making your connections aware of current happenings at your school is as easy as posting an update on your LinkedIn profile. You might

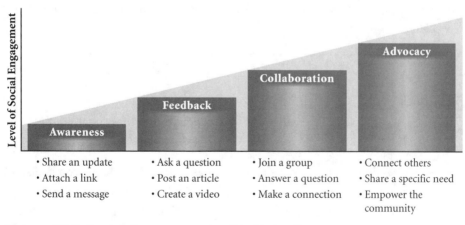

Figure 13.2 Social Engagement with LinkedIn

post, for example, "Tonight we are hosting an open house at our school. To learn more, click here," combined with a link that leads visitors to a Facebook event with details including the time, the place, and other information required for attendees.

- **Attach a link.** Another way to build awareness about your school is to share a link on LinkedIn. You can do this by posting the link as an update on your profile or by sending a message to a specific connection. The link could be an online news article about your school, a YouTube video that conveys your school's mission, or a research article pertinent to your school's philosophy or pedagogical approach.

- **Send a message.** A third way to build awareness about your school is to send a message to your connections. For example, let's say one of your connections works for a chemical company. Send a personal message inviting her to your school to attend the student science fair.

Linking LinkedIn

Many social media tools are built to share content and updates from one tool to another automatically. Using Ping.fm, you can link multiple social media accounts together. This way you can write one status update, and LinkedIn, Twitter, and Facebook will all be updated at the same time. Another tool you may want to use is HootSuite, an online social media dashboard that helps you manage social media accounts in one convenient place.

Feedback

There are several ways to receive feedback from your professional connections on LinkedIn:

- **Ask a question.** You can pose a question as a status update, or you can send a question to a specific person. For example, "What do you think about . . . ?" Whatever your question, you encourage feedback from your professional connections.

- **Post an article with a comment or question.** This is a noninvasive way for you to reach out to your professional connections. For example, post a link to a *New York Times* article, and ask, "What do you think about this article?" This may result in your connections' offering their feedback, allowing you to gauge your network's thoughts or opinions on a topic.

- **Upload a video to your profile.** People like to watch videos, and they are more likely to view your video than to read an article or click on an external link. The video does not have to be professionally produced. It can be as simple as you looking into the camera, speaking about your experiences, and posing questions to your connections. Your connections can comment on your video or send you a direct message in response.

Collaboration

LinkedIn is a great tool for collaborating with your professional network. There are several ways to build collaboration across your professional network to increase the social engagement in your school.

- **Join a LinkedIn group.** Members receive updates each time a new comment is posted in their LinkedIn group. This allows you to have an ongoing conversation with other professionals interested in the same topic. There are LinkedIn groups for academic subject areas, technology topics, specific job functions, and a growing list of professional organizations.

- **Answer questions.** Add to the community dialogue and show that you are interested in other professionals by answering questions posted on LinkedIn. The more value you add for your connections, the more willing they will be to engage with your school community.

- **Make connections.** Find ways to introduce members of your network to each other. You will be seen as an individual who takes an interest in others. The goodwill you earn through these acts can have an impact on your school in limitless positive ways.

Advocacy

LinkedIn is a great tool for increasing advocacy for your school. Here are three specific ways to help empower your professional connections to advocate for your school.

- **Introduce your students.** Student success stories are your greatest tool to empower others to advocate for your school. Share these success stories, and introduce your students to your connections. Powerful stories naturally spread across networks.

- **Share specific needs.** Professionals on LinkedIn are usually willing to share content when they feel that they can make a difference. Inviting members of your community to contribute to your school in a specific way will encourage them to forward your need to others in their network, resulting in a wider reach for your message.

- **Empower your community.** Consider the tools and resources your supporters will need to advocate for your school. When a connection on LinkedIn asks, "How can I help out?" answer with one of the following:
  - "Can you put up this poster at your office?"
  - "Can you hand out these postcards to your colleagues?"
  - "Can you forward this e-mail to your connections?"

Be prepared by being specific in what you are asking for and ensure that when a connection on LinkedIn offers to advocate for your school you can deliver the resources she will need to spread your message.

HIRING GREAT TEACHERS BEFORE AND AFTER LINKEDIN

There are several ways to hire great faculty and staff on LinkedIn. As the leader of a charter start-up, I had difficulty finding the right mix of novice and experienced teachers to establish the school culture during our first year. After discovering the power of recruiting on LinkedIn, I was able to specifically target individual instructors through their LinkedIn profile. The table that follows outlines how you can use LinkedIn to recruit great teachers.

Education blogger Jeff Dunn of Edudemic believes that LinkedIn is a great resource for teachers and educators to connect with one another. "LinkedIn is huge with teachers and education professionals. According to today's release from the social network, there are now more than 100 million users on LinkedIn. Just how many of those are teachers? Turns out a LOT. Nearly 1 million teachers are currently using the service."

"How Many Teachers Use LinkedIn? The Official Answer Is In," accessed December 3, 2011, http://edudemic.com/2011/03/linkedin-teachers/.

Task or Goal	Traditional Method	Using LinkedIn
Posting a job announcement	You would run a classified ad in the newspaper.	You can post an update to your profile announcing the job opening and create a targeted LinkedIn ad that only qualified applicants will see.
Searching for quality staff	You would ask people you know if they had any leads.	You can search LinkedIn using the built-in people search.
Reaching out to a specific school	You would visit the school in person.	You can locate the school's organization page and view the school's connections.
Asking for referrals	You would use the phone or e-mail to reach out to colleagues.	You can reach out to your LinkedIn network.
Viewing recommendation letters	You would wait to receive recommendation letters in the mail or via e-mail.	You can view recommendations on the candidate's LinkedIn profile.
Announcing the new hire	You would announce the new hire in your photocopied school newsletter and post the information on your school website.	The new hire updates his or her LinkedIn profile.

LINKEDIN BEST PRACTICES

To use a professional networking site such as LinkedIn most effectively, follow these etiquette tips and best practices. If you follow three simple rules—provide value, connect professionally, and reply promptly and appropriately—you'll build a solid reputation and a network that engages connections across other networks and sets you apart as a thought leader.

Provide Value

Give before you take, and deposit before you withdraw. Savvy school leaders know that before making a negative phone call to a parent, it is always a good idea to have established a positive relationship. Find ways to say something positive before you criticize. The same is true of social networks. Before you ask for something, always give. Your contacts need to be wooed. Become the person who provides value to your network. Four ways to offer value on LinkedIn are to share great content, write recommendations, connect others, and stay current.

Share Great Content

Add links to articles, videos, blogs, and professional resources that you feel would benefit your connections. If you regularly and frequently share valuable content, your connections will see you as a resource for information. When they need assistance, they will turn to you for help. One strategy to share great content is to read with a purpose. Think of all of the social news tools available for sharing information and articles—when you are reading the *New York Times* or *Education Week* and you find something interesting, instead of just highlighting the article or photocopying it for your faculty, consider who in your LinkedIn network would also benefit from the article. Send these connections a message on LinkedIn, saying, "You might want to check this out. This might be helpful to you because . . ." Make this a daily habit. When the time comes to ask for something, you will be seen as someone who provides value, and others will return the favor.

Write Recommendations

Use LinkedIn to recommend those with whom you have worked in the past. Writing short recommendations on LinkedIn only takes a few minutes and has a strong impact on others. This is a great way to provide value to your connections without asking for anything. Often your generosity will be reciprocated. As an added bonus, others who read the recommendation will click the link to your page and learn more about you and your school.

Connect Others

Set yourself apart professionally by building relationships between your connections. Look at the list of people you know, considering how they might be of value to one another. Make an introduction between two of your connections, expressing the mutual benefit they'll receive. Becoming a connector invites others to connect with you.

Stay Current

Make it easy for your connections to stay engaged with your professional work. This is as simple as posting a status update once a week that shares your excitement about a current project. Seeing LinkedIn as part of your professional practice will help you both increase your brand equity and grow professionally. The worst time to network for a new position is when you don't have one, and the best time to network is when you are happy with your current position. Become a frequent LinkedIn updater. Establish a regular routine of posting a link to a favorite article once a week. If you are just getting started with LinkedIn, simply set a scheduled reminder on your calendar tool or mobile device for Friday morning to visit three educational websites, read through five or so articles, and post a link to one that seems interesting. This regular routine of posting links to interesting articles will help your content stay in front of your connections.

Connect Professionally

LinkedIn is an amazing tool for building your professional network. You can connect to anyone in the world, including some heavyweights in your field. You need to be careful, however, with how you reach out to new connections. Sending an unsolicited e-mail to someone whom you don't know, even if you are not trying to sell anything, is often seen as spam. This is not an effective method for developing relationships. Instead of bulk uploading a list of e-mail addresses, build your network authentically by following these steps: reach out in a timely way,

> *LinkedIn features many professional networking groups for principals and teachers to discuss issues they face and find collaborative solutions. An example is the Principals and Teachers Network founded by Stephen Jones, an educational consultant in Philadelphia. The group features over 1,100 members.*
>
> "Principals and Teachers Network, accessed May 2, 2012, www.linkedin.com/groups /Principals-Teachers-Network-1933849.

send personalized invitations, provide value after acceptance, follow up, and be gracious if you don't hear back.

Reach Out in a Timely Way

Before a conference, after a conference, after receiving a business card, or after meeting at an event are all ideal times to connect on LinkedIn. Make it a regular part of your evening routine. After returning home, while removing business cards from your pockets, log on and invite the people you have just met to connect with you on LinkedIn. Best practices indicate a forty-eight-hour window to effectively make this connection.

Send Personalized Invitations

Write a personalized LinkedIn invitation. Although LinkedIn has a standard connection invitation, I recommend customizing this message to fit your personality and the nature of the relationship with the person with whom you are connecting. Even a personal note such as "Hope you're doing well. Looking forward to connecting with you on LinkedIn" is better than the stock e-mail. A personalized request always stands out from the crowd.

Provide Value After Acceptance

Once a person accepts you as a connection, write him back and send a link to content that he might find valuable, stating, "John, thanks for connecting on LinkedIn. Here is a link to an article you may able to use." Once you've heard back from that contact, feel free to begin a conversation. Find ways to engage in a two-way conversation rather than a one-way solicitation. For example, ask what he thought of the article you sent to him.

Follow Up

Ensure that there are multiple times when you make contact with your new connection. These "touch points" will assist you in cementing your position as a valuable resource for that new connection.

Be Gracious If You Don't Hear Back

Always give people the benefit of the doubt and the opportunity to respond. The novice LinkedIn user probably receives a daily message from the site, depending on that person's LinkedIn settings and preferences. These are easy to ignore. Your message could be perceived in the same way and might simply be ignored. Remember that people are busy. Be patient, yet tenacious. If you haven't heard back from someone in a reasonable amount of time, forward your original e-mail, stating, "I know you're busy, but you've got to check this out." This tenacity can be a positive attribute. Saying it in a nice way establishes rapport and mutual respect. If your connection is someone you know, she'll probably write you back.

Reply Promptly and Appropriately

As you begin to engage in professional dialogue on LinkedIn, you will receive direct messages to which you will need to respond. Four ways to ensure you reply promptly and appropriately are to establish a follow-up policy, schedule replies, show gratitude, and take the conversation offline.

- **Establish a follow-up policy.** Establish a follow-up policy, directly responding to others within twenty-four to forty-eight hours of receiving their message.

- **Schedule replies.** Schedule a specific time to process your e-mail each day. Include responding to LinkedIn messages as part of that follow-up process.

- **Show gratitude.** When someone connects you to a luminary in your field, give him credit and make sure to thank him for the connection. Although it is true that social media is an equalizer, it is still important to show respect and give credit where credit is due. Build a reputation for generosity, and notables will begin to reach out to you.

- **Take the conversation offline.** If it is a person whom you know, feel free to follow up with a personal e-mail or a phone call. Even though LinkedIn is a great tool for networking, there is something to be said for the traditional phone call. Because we receive so many e-mails now and much fewer phone calls, personal touches stand out. Sending a handwritten note on your personal stationary goes a step beyond and adds lasting value to the relationship.

NEXT-LEVEL LINKEDIN

Once you have mastered using LinkedIn for your own professional networking, here are three additional ways to use this tool beyond engaging your current connections. These strategies include establishing your school's organization page, creating LinkedIn ads, and engaging donors and community members.

Establishing Your School's Organization Page

Begin by creating your school's profile on LinkedIn. Each organization has the opportunity to create a presence on LinkedIn, and, as a school leader, you can establish that presence. If you are at a district or charter organization, work with the communication department to establish a LinkedIn page for your school. Any school has current and former employees, so before you start making personal connections, get your school's page off the ground. Others will say that they have been a former or current employee, and word of your school's LinkedIn page will spread. Seeing an organization on LinkedIn will allow others to find out more about your school on their own.

Creating LinkedIn Ads

LinkedIn offers a pay-per-click ad feature to help you advertise open positions. As you might with other social media ads, such as those on Twitter and Facebook, you can target specific users by region, education level, and other factors. This tool may be worth an investigation by your human resources department.

Engaging Donors and Community Members

LinkedIn is the perfect tool to engage donors and community members in your school's efforts. Many business owners and community leaders who don't take the time to follow your school website may be willing to engage with you on LinkedIn to build their own professional practice. You can use this connection to begin to plant seeds about your school. Once relationships have been established, you have the opportunity to begin to engage them as potential donors and community volunteers.

My favorite way to engage donors is to have them serve on project panels, allowing them to see the work that our students are doing firsthand. This is called a "soft ask." Once a potential donor is excited about the work at your school, continue to invite him or her into deeper conversations about your school and its needs. Staying connected on LinkedIn is a noninvasive way to build relationships with community volunteers and donors.

GETTING STARTED WITH LINKEDIN

Question for Reflection: What actions and conversations would need to take place for you to use LinkedIn to recruit next year's teachers?

First Steps

1. After completing a positive classroom observation, post a recommendation for that teacher on LinkedIn. Unsolicited recommendations often inspire very thankful staff.

2. I would like to offer a personal invitation to connect with me on LinkedIn. After you've signed up for an account, visit linkedin.com/in/drbrianjdixon to add me as a connection. You'll be able to visit my profile, view my reading list, and receive access to a bonus training video on using LinkedIn with your students. I look forward to connecting with you!

Google+

This chapter explores Google+ (or Google Plus), a collection of social media tools recently launched by Google. You will learn specific methods to take full advantage of the features of these innovative tools. Topics include

- What is Google+?
- Google+ features
- Ongoing social engagement with Google+
- Common school tasks before and after Google+
- Getting started with Google+

WHAT IS GOOGLE+?

Google+ is the latest social networking offering by the Internet search giant Google. It integrates many of the best tools for online collaboration into one product. Just like many other online tools, Google+ is completely free. Only launched in 2011, Google+ is quickly becoming one of the key online networks for school leaders to use. What makes Google+ stand out from its competitors, chiefly Facebook, is the number of tools integrated into one system.

There are four main reasons to consider using Google+:

- **Integrated tools.** Google+ unifies the power of multiple social media tools within one site. One single log-in. One main place to visit all of these tools available to you.

- **Google Docs integration.** Google+ seamlessly integrates with Gmail, Google Docs, Google Sites, and Google Calendar.

- **Network segmentation.** Google+ segments your network into different groupings for sharing applicable content. This means that you can use Google+ for your personal relationships—such as by updating family photos and communicating with your family—separate from communicating with your work colleagues.

- **Further reach.** A large percentage of Internet users already use Gmail and Google Calendar, and Google+ is now part of that system. This is a growing network of audience members for your school's content. By using Google+, you can make your content and your school's message a part of those users' social stream and social experience. You want to capitalize on that. You want to be where the viewers are. If your school families and your community are using Google+, then you want to make sure that your school is also using Google+.

GOOGLE+ FEATURES

As an integrated system of social media tools, Google+ offers many features for users to engage with their community online. These tools range from user profiles and a newsfeed to features that enable posting photos and hosting video conversations.

Profiles

Establishing a basic Google+ profile is similar to setting up a Facebook profile, whereby you create your own page on the Internet by uploading your basic contact information, status updates, photos and videos, and different places on the Internet that you have said you liked. Most mainstream websites are now using Google's +1 feature. When you are visiting a website and are reading an article that you like, you can click the "+1" button, and this page will automatically be added to your Google+ profile. This helps you save great content that you have seen online and share it with your connections so that you can better communicate your passions and interests to your group of friends.

Stream

A stream is a newsfeed on the main page. A stream is similar to the Facebook newsfeed in that you receive regular updates from your various connections on Google+. You can see what people are doing, what they are interested in, what articles they are reading, what photos they have posted, and what videos they like.

Sparks

Sparks is a newer tool that has fascinating educational applications. It's a recommendation engine, based on topics. A spark on a particular topic helps others who are looking for information on that topic learn more. For example, if you created a spark of classroom management strategies, you might include various links and content on that spark. Other people can visit that spark and add their own feedback and ideas. Over time, this content will become highly valuable and beneficial to the readers. A spark is basically a dedicated page of curated information on niche topics, which you can simply read or to which you can contribute. The Sparks tool is similar in many ways to a competitor called Squidoo, through which people create lenses, or online pages, that outline the basic ideas of any main concept. For example, a lens might offer the best digital SLR cameras available today by price point.

Hangouts

One of the most fascinating tools offered by Google+ is Hangouts, which allows you to schedule a group video conversation that you can invite others to join. As long as you have a webcam on your computer, you can have an instant conversation with others online. Hangouts is a great tool for collaboration, allowing you to network with other educational leaders by having authentic conversations. Hangouts could replace the traditional meeting as we know it. It offers all of the benefits of a face-to-face meeting (reading facial expressions, listening to the tone of voice, seeing people react to what you are saying) without the travel. This will serve educational leaders better than the traditional Web conference, or teleconference, in that the transparency and authenticity of online video—and face-to-face conversation—will help increase engagement and will ultimately lead to better understanding. Hangouts is similar to Skype, but it's more social in that you can host a hangout, establishing the time when you will be discussing a particular topic and inviting your friends to join you in a video conversation on that topic.

> On his Google+ profile, Mark Lewis, associate professor at Trinity University, explains how he uses this tool to engage students. "I use Google+ to share ideas with people, including students. I also find hangouts to be a nice way to "meet" with students when I can't be on campus."
>
> "Mark Lewis," accessed April 23, 2012, https://plus.google.com/100654668159184005181/about.

Huddle

Another feature is Huddle, which lets you send group text messages to multiple people. This can be useful for communicating a simple message to all faculty or all parents. You could also "huddle" with teachers, sending out a group message informing your teaching staff of a change to the schedule or updates on the school observation team's location. Each faculty member will receive the messages on his or her cell phone, helping everyone stay on the same page, similar to a team huddle before a play during a football game. Huddle up!

Circles

Circles is a platform that allows you to categorize your connections into specific groups, such as family, work friends, and personal friends. You can then share specific information with that select group. Circles is, perhaps, the best innovation of Google+. You can share specific resources with a targeted group of people. No longer will you post an article on classroom management that your uncle will also see on your Facebook profile. Now you can share educational content selectively with other educators in your Google+ circle. Other school administrators with whom you collaborate no longer have to see your baby photos or pictures from a night out with friends, because you can choose to only share those personal photos with your family circle and your friends circle, respectively. The basic idea is that a conversation is never intended for everyone to hear. The tone, the content, and the audience are completely different depending on the social group with which we are communicating. Circles is one of the first technological steps in personalizing and segmenting our social networking communication online.

Photos

Photos is a photo sharing service similar to Google's Picasa, allowing you to upload and archive your photos with unlimited bandwidth and memory. Many of these features are available other places on the Internet, with Facebook being a main competitor, but with Google+ you can easily choose who can and can't see which photos.

> Education blogger Marina Salsbury of Edudemic illustrates that Google+'s ability to organize users into circles allows for clean organization and distribution of information. "Google+'s Sparks feature allows users to mark articles, blogs, and other information relevant to topics of interest, and label each group of websites according to their topics. Share each group of topics with people in particular circles, and Google+ becomes a project and research-sharing tool useful to any classroom."
>
> "Where Does Google+ Fit in Education?" posted October 13, 2011, http://edudemic.com/2011/10/google-plus-education/.

Integration

What truly makes Google+ fascinating is not the individual tools—it's that Google brings all of these tools together. If your school has adopted Google Apps (including Gmail, Google Calendar, Google Docs, and Google Sites), Google+ is now added to that central online toolbox. Google can be your one main place on the Internet to check your e-mail; update your calendar; see what is happening with your friends; share an online article; post your photos; and communicate with parents, faculty, and other professional connections.

ONGOING SOCIAL ENGAGEMENT WITH GOOGLE+

Google+ can help build ongoing social engagement online (see Figure 14.1). The many tools built into Google+ make it the perfect platform for sharing your message and building engagement across your school community.

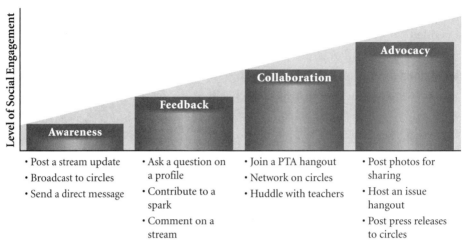

Figure 14.1 Social Engagement with Google+

Awareness

Google+ lets you set up a business page, which will help spread awareness about your school. You can post recent updates, news, and information similar to what you would post on Twitter or Facebook. Many tools talk to each other within Google+. Updating your status on one tool that integrates with the others will help ensure that members of your school community are informed of the latest school news, no matter what social media tool (Facebook, Google+, Twitter) they primarily use. It is your job, as a school leader, to make sure that you are communicating with your school community. The farther and wider you spread your content, the more potential you have in engaging every parent, student, and community member. You can use Google+ to spread awareness, for example, by posting a stream update, broadcasting to your circles, and sending a direct message to someone else to whom you are connected on Google+.

Feedback

Google+ is also a great tool for receiving feedback from your school community. By posting a status update or a link to an article, you can receive +1s, which will show you who likes your content. And, if they have something to add to the conversation, they can also respond with a comment. You can also receive feedback by asking a question on a stream update, contributing content to a spark, and commenting on another user's stream.

Collaboration

Here are a few specific ways to build collaboration using Google+. You can schedule a hangout with your parent-teacher association, create a professional networking group with Circles, and join a huddle with a group of teachers. Authentic online collaboration that matches the power of face-to-face conversation is now in sight. Imagine having parent conferences through Hangouts. A student's two concerned teachers, the guidance counselor, and both parents can attend a videoconference in real time, for free, through one click, without having to be in the same building. This tool could be very powerful for ensuring that you are on the same page with your school families. It is also a great tool for building collaboration in that you can have authentic conversations with the planning team of an annual fundraiser or with the PTA. Because these hangouts are held online, they can be archived through screen recording. Sharing these conversations with the PTA or school board, for example, can give viewers a sense of these meetings' tone.

Advocacy

Google+ is a great tool for building advocacy because it allows other users to spread content. Adding a "+1" button to the articles on your page enables your school community to indicate that they like your content. Every time other users do this for your school content, it is added to their stream, which means that their connections will see your articles, announcements, and events, helping spread the message from your network to theirs. Three specific ways to encourage advocacy using Google+ are to share photos from school events, host a hangout to discuss school policies and issues, and post school press releases or board meeting notices to your circles.

COMMON SCHOOL TASKS BEFORE AND AFTER GOOGLE+

Google+ can change the way you complete common school tasks, such as hosting weekly book talks, arranging parent conferences, and communicating with your team.

Task or Goal	Traditional Method	Using Google+
Hosting weekly book talks	A book club meeting would have to be set at a certain date and time on campus. Faculty might read the book to prepare, and then be unable to attend at the last minute.	With Hangouts, a day and time can be arranged when everyone who read the book can discuss it online. People can easily join the discussion late and can still participate if they couldn't find a babysitter.
Arranging parent conferences	The parents would have to be contacted with a phone call or through a note sent home with their child. All parents would have to try to meet with the teacher on the same weeknight.	With Hangouts, teachers can set up convenient times to meet individually with parents online. These meetings can easily be spread out over a week or two. Parents will feel more comfortable because it will seem like the teacher is dedicating that slot of time specifically to them and their student.
Communicating an important message to your team	If a bus was running late, or if an assembly had been rescheduled, an announcement would be made over the intercom, disrupting every class in the school.	With Huddle, a group text message can be sent to all faculty to alert them of the schedule changes. They can check the text message without interrupting class and can share the announcement with students when it's convenient.

GETTING STARTED WITH GOOGLE+

Questions for Reflection: What surprised you about Google+? Which feature holds the most potential for your faculty team?

First Steps

1. Sign up for Google+ if you haven't already. Start with one tool, perhaps Hangouts, to begin using this powerful social media platform.

2. Visit YouTube and search for "Google+ training." The videos you find will help you learn to use Google+ much faster than you would by using trial and error.

Your Online Presence

This chapter focuses on specific strategies for building your online presence to help your school become more visible online. The topics covered are

- Improving your Web visibility
- Strategies to increase your online presence
- Managing your school's reputation online
- Using location-based tools
- Getting started with your online presence

IMPROVING YOUR WEB VISIBILITY

When someone googles the name of your school, you want your school to be the first result that they see. It doesn't matter how great your online content is if your target audience cannot locate you online through a basic search. Appearing in the first few results of an online search is important to school leaders for several reasons, including

> It is critical for your website to appear at or near the top of Google search engine results for your school name. A recent study showed that the number one search result receives over one-third of all visitor clicks. Less than 12 percent of users click to the second page of results to find what they are looking for online.
>
> "Top Google Result Gets 36.4% of Clicks [Study]," posted April 21, 2011, http://searchenginewatch.com/article/2049695/Top-Google-Result-Gets-36.4-of-Clicks-Study.

- **Convenience.** You want your school community to find information quickly and easily. The more you build your online presence, the easier it is for them to engage with you.

- **Admissions.** For schools that compete for student admissions (and it can be argued that all of them do), ensuring that your school is the first to appear will help establish your school as *the* school to attend.

- **Teacher recruiting.** The same theory applies for hiring great teachers. When teachers are looking for a new teaching position, they often search on Google for available opportunities. Ensuring that your site appears in the first few results will improve your chances of engaging these candidates.

- **Fundraising and donations.** If someone searches for a school in your area, you want yours to be the first one to show up. An expanded online presence may help set up your school for funding, as establishing a strong presence online leads to greater awareness, which may lead to donations.

STRATEGIES TO INCREASE YOUR ONLINE PRESENCE

Improving your school's visibility online is possible by following a few proven steps. These include frequently posting content online, using the same username across networks, and widely distributing content. Implementing these strategies will increase your school's online presence, helping to engage current members of your school community and build relationships with a larger audience unfamiliar with your school.

Frequently Posting Relevant Content

The key strategy to ensuring that your school is easy to find online is to continually post relevant, high-quality, and properly categorized and tagged content. Start by frequently posting news and updated stories on your school website. Be sure to include links to other websites and news sources directly in your site's articles to build connections. Next, ensure that you provide readable and high-quality content so that more people will visit and interact with it. Use the categories feature of your content management system to assign categories to each of your posts and pages. Our categories (as shown in Figure 15.1) are based on the design principles of our school, which include

- Project-based learning
- Technology integration
- Mentoring relationships

Categorizing our content in this way helps add structure and hierarchy to our school website, and it also helps our website map appear in search results in an organized fashion. Your website map refers to the way your site's content is indexed by such search engines as Google and Bing. The more organized your website content is, the clearer your search results will appear.

Figure 15.1 Screenshot: Website Categories

Unifying Domain Names and Usernames

Build natural connections online by adopting a clear naming structure for all of your domain names and usernames. Depending on your school name, it is very likely that there are other schools in different cities that share this name. Although location-based search is starting to help solve this problem, it is still not uncommon for a Google search to display the results of both your school and another school with the same name in a different area of the country. Create a unique naming structure to help your school stand out. Our school's username, for example, is mentorshipbr (with "br" for Baton Rouge). Although there may be other mentorship programs, we are the number one mentorshipbr. Googling this unique word that we created will immediately direct the searcher to our content. To unify usernames, be sure that you choose a unique username that is short and memorable, embodies your school spirit, and is available on the majority of social networks.

Finding the Perfect Domain Name and Username

There are a few general rules about selecting both domain names and usernames to help identify your school online. Our domain name is where our website is located—mentorshipbr.org—whereas our username on sites such as Twitter is mentorshipbr. Keeping your names to fifteen characters or fewer fits the rules of every major social media site. Let's say, for example, that your school name is Greendale. You could be facebook.com/Greendale, twitter.com/Greendale, Greendale.org, and so on. All of your teachers could have e-mail addresses at theirname@Greendale.org. It's clean, it's neat, it's easily searchable, and your school becomes easier to find online because the name is simple. Unfortunately, given that it only costs about eight dollars a year to maintain a domain name, Greendale .org is already taken by another school. The same will likely be true for your school name as well. So, get a little creative. If your school happens to be Greendale Regional High School, consider how you can shorten that name into a unique handle. Brainstorm on a piece of paper: GreendaleHS, GreendaleRH (with "RH" for Regional High), or GreendaleRHS. Maybe there's a nickname you could use. If your team name is the Greendale Spartans, you could go with Greenspartans.org. Find ways to make your domain name stand out but be easily remembered.

One of my favorite tools is called Domainr, a name suggestion service. You type in your URL idea plus your website name idea, and Domainr gives you suggestions on how to shorten your domain name or how to spell it differently. Some of the suggestions are a little out there, but they might help inspire you to find your right domain name. With Greendale Regional High School we settled on GDRHS. GDRHS.org was available, as were facebook.com/GDRHS and twitter.com/GDRHS.

Signing Up for Multiple Social Networks

Use your username to register for as many social networks as possible to maintain uniformity. Start by creating a username that you can use across multiple networks. NameChk lets you see if your desired username or vanity URL is available at numerous social networking and social bookmarking websites (see Figure 15.2). Before you sign up for an account on a site such as Twitter, use NameChk to see which usernames are available across most popular networks. Try searching multiple names to find one that's available on the majority of social networking sites. Even if you aren't planning on using them right away, sign up for multiple social media services just in case members of your audience begin to use those services in the future.

Protecting Your Domain Name

One new area of responsibility for a school leader involves protecting the school's domain name. When we first launched our school, we actually used domain

Figure 15.2 Screenshot: NameChk

names as one of the factors in selecting our school name. As Mentorship Academy, we wanted to buy MentorshipAcademy.org. If MentorshipAcademy.org had been taken, we would have seriously considered renaming our school; it's that important. Your school, even if it's a district school, deserves to have its own domain name. We mostly use mentorshipbr.org with the idea that eventually we could also be mentorshipga.org or mentorshipnola.org. NameChk will also automatically sign up for domains for you, so when a hot new social network pops up, you can be assured that NameChk will reserve your username on that new network.

Widely Distributing Content

To help your school be visible and become more recognized, distribute your content as far and as wide as possible. This means using as many social media platforms and places on the Internet as possible. This is the new search engine optimization. When your content is showing up in multiple places, all leading back to your school website, and someone researches your school name, your school is likely to be displayed at the top of the search results. Even schools with a very common name, like Washington High School, can help to increase their search engine ranking by using multiple social media platforms.

Using automatic multiposting services, such as Ping.fm or TubeMogul, will ensure that your content appears in multiple places. All of these places link back to your website. Every time someone clicks on a new link from a different location, this will help raise the visibility of your website. Whenever you send out an e-mail, an eNewsletter, or a link to anybody, always include a link back to your site. This practice alone can dramatically increase your ranking in search engines.

Getting Started with Ping.fm

Instead of updating your status directly on Twitter or Facebook, you can post your status to Ping.fm. Your status then will automatically show up on all of your networks. Ping.fm allows for two different types of posts: microblogs and blog posts. Microblogs are treated as status updates, for example on Facebook and Twitter. Blog posts are longer content pieces treated as online articles for WordPress and the notes section of Facebook. Your status updates appear on all of the services that you have signed up for. This way, your students who use Bebo will be able to see the same updates as your students who still use MySpace. Even if it engages only one more student to sign up for accounts on all of the available social networking sites, it is worth the couple of minutes it takes to sign up for the account. Then, with Ping.fm, it's easy to update accounts regularly to maintain engagement.

To get started with Ping.fm, you should

1. **Sign up for multiple networks.** Ensure you know the username and password for such sites as Facebook and Twitter. We use one e-mail address and a unified password for our social networks to keep this easy.

2. **Create an account on Ping.fm.** Following the same naming conventions as discussed earlier, we used ping@MentorshipAcademy.org to sign up for our Ping.fm account.

3. **Set up multiposting.** Click each social network listed and enter your log-in credentials (username and password) to connect all of your networks to start pinging!

Linking Social Media Accounts

If you would like to keep it simple and only post on the major sites, you can still link accounts. Facebook can link to Twitter, and then anytime you update your Facebook page, Twitter is automatically updated and vice versa. Linking accounts is an intelligent way to update your status on multiple platforms. When accounts are linked, that status update appears once on each account.

Advanced Tip   A custom URL shortener available through Bit.ly will take a long Web address and shorten it to something that makes it easier to remember and thus share. When you share a link in an e-mail, it's better to have a short link so it doesn't get "truncated" or knocked down to the next line. By shortening a domain name, you make it easier to share with others, and Bit.ly readily allows you to do this. Simply take any URL and paste it into the box on Bit.ly, and you'll receive your shortened address in seconds.

Creating a Catch-All E-Mail Account

Use a catch-all e-mail account to sign up for these services. A catch-all account will forward e-mails sent to an inactive e-mail address at your domain name to an e-mail address of your choosing. A catch-all account allows us to redirect e-mail messages to specified people instead of creating an unreasonable number of e-mail accounts. Our facebook@MentorshipAcademy.org, for example, is automatically forwarded to our technology coordinator, who manages our Facebook page. E-mails sent to youtube@MentorshipAcademy.org are forwarded to our digital media teacher, who also manages our YouTube account. We use catch-all e-mail accounts instead of signing up using a specific person's name so that when a staff member changes positions, we don't have to log on to each social network to change the username.

Managing Passwords

The password that we use always includes the first initial of the given domain name. For example, a Facebook password would start with an "F," and a Twitter password would start with a "T." This letter is followed by a random phrase, a number, and some sort of punctuation—for example, "fpanda57!" or "tgreenhouse19?" This password strategy meets the criteria of most social media platforms. It is also a lot easier than having to remember a different password for every social media account.

Always Linking to Your Homepage

Whenever you post on Facebook, Twitter, or any other site, always include a link back to your school website—your anchor site online. Make sure that your website is link friendly, such as GreendaleHighSchool.com. These links back will help your school appear higher in the search engine rankings.

MANAGING YOUR SCHOOL'S REPUTATION ONLINE

Expanding your online presence is more than pushing your content out into the world. You also need to know when and where your school is being mentioned online. The sooner you are notified, the quicker you can respond. There are a few services that will tell you when your school has been mentioned. If, for example, a blog has mentioned your school as an example of an institution that effectively uses technology, it would be to your advantage to be aware of that blog post and perhaps use it in your eNewsletter or include a link to it on your website.

Besides physically searching for your school name, you can set up a Google alert to automatically notify you anytime your school has been mentioned on your social networks. This will allow you a chance to respond. If a news article is written about your school, for example, you will be notified when the article is posted to that newspaper's website. You receive an e-mail alert, and you can click on the link and perhaps comment on that article. This comment should include a link back to your website, inviting those who read the article to further engage with your school. This allows you to extend the media coverage you are receiving. If, however, the media coverage is negative, a Google alert can help you respond to that coverage, commenting on the article to explain your position or defend your school's actions and including a link for more information. Social media is all about finding ways to engage in the conversation in a timely manner.

USING LOCATION-BASED TOOLS

People use technology to find information and make connections. Although much of this book is about increasing connections in the online space, it is also important to be able to have people find your school in real life. Several tools exist to help people find your school, the major one being Google Maps.

When someone is planning on visiting your school and wants to know where your school is located, he or she is very likely to google the name of your school. If you create a Google Places account, your school's location will appear in the Google search results with a link to an interactive map. When visitors click on the icon of your school on the map, they will see more than just the school name and address. Using Google Places, you can post photos that will appear on Google Maps, your phone number, your office hours, a short description of your school, and a link to your website (see Figure 15.3). This will allow the first-time visitors to get to know a lot more about your school than just your location. Other location-based tools exist, such as Facebook Places, FourSquare, and Gowalla. It can't be said enough: the more networks that your school uses, the more you will get your content out to your potential audience.

Figure 15.3 Screenshot: Google Maps

GETTING STARTED WITH YOUR ONLINE PRESENCE

Question for Reflection: Would your school website be easy to find if you were new to the area and had just performed a Google search?

First Steps

1. Perform a Google search for your school. Click on the Google Maps listing to see what information is present.

2. Sign up for a Google Places account to update your school's listing on Google Maps.

3. Use NameChk to search for your school's username on multiple social networks.

Social Media in Practice

One of the key features of social media is that many of the tools work together to help your message connect with as many people as possible. To show how social media tools come together, this chapter presents three case studies demonstrating how a model school integrates all of the available social media tools. Case studies include

- Promoting a schoolwide community service day
- Recruiting, screening, and hiring teachers
- Grant funding with social media
- Soliciting donations with social media
- Getting started with social media

These case studies are detailed accounts that will convince even the most skeptical school leaders to see the value of integrating social media into their daily practice.

PROMOTING A SCHOOLWIDE COMMUNITY SERVICE DAY

Any school has events and activities that have an impact on a larger audience than the school campus. These often involve a lot of moving pieces that need to be managed, including invitations, contracts, phone calls, schedules, transportation, and other logistics. This section focuses on a schoolwide community service day that we hosted at Mentorship Academy. Each of the social media tools covered in this book were used in one way or another to announce, schedule, and share this day of community service.

The Event

We partnered with eleven nonprofits in the Greater Baton Rouge area to create a service learning opportunity for our students. We wanted each and every one of our students to experience the service learning day by doing the following:

- Learning about their assigned nonprofit
- Developing their communication skills
- Documenting their process in serving the community
- Sharing their experience with other students, parents, and the community

Here is how we used social media before, during, and after the day to keep families and the community included in the conversation.

Planning the Event

Before assigning students to nonprofits, we used an **online survey form** to gauge student interest in specific causes. This helped us know which nonprofits to reach out to based on our students' genuine interests. We also used an online survey form for nonprofits interested in partnering with us.

Our initial **e-mail** to the selected nonprofits included some basic information about our school as well as links to our **school website** and **social media** pages. This allowed us to establish credibility with these potential partners, who were then able to learn much more about our school through photos, videos, articles, and status updates on our social media pages.

Announcing the Event

Once the volunteer opportunities had been set up, we began to promote the service learning day. We started by announcing the event to families in our weekly **eNewsletter,** a link to which we posted on the main page of our **school website.** We posted the date of the event with **Ping.fm,** automatically updating all of our networks, including **Facebook** and **Twitter.**

We began a discussion topic on **Ning** to get students excited for the event and to get their feedback. Students also created a "service learning" section on their **student portfolio** to begin blogging about the event.

As the school leader, I created a video about the service learning day and posted it on my **blog** and **YouTube** account. This video and the mention in our **eNewsletter** helped us recruit volunteers to help with the logistics.

We used **Constant Contact** to send our **eNewsletter** announcing the event to our parents, and we posted a printable copy of the permission form on the parent group on **Ning** for parents to fill out, sign, and send in.

Scheduling the Event

Several tools were used to help schedule the day and manage communication throughout. First, we used **Doodle** to schedule the best times to meet as a team for our planning meetings. Doodle is a collaborative tool for setting appointments, allowing multiple users to state their availability and then select a time based on the schedule of the whole group. Next, we used **Google Calendar** to schedule the event and communicate important times. Finally, during the event itself we used our **mobile devices,** including our cell phones, to text message each other to coordinate bus delays and food service information.

Sharing the Event

Using press releases, **Twitter** updates, **eNewsletters,** and direct messages, we were able to get coverage in the local media, both on TV and in the newspaper. Don't forget to use traditional media, such as the TV news media and printed newspapers, to share your school's story. These are also great resources for gathering content to post to your **social media** networks.

> **Tip** Make friends with the video editor at the news station, as this person will be able to provide you with a high-quality, high-definition video file on a USB drive. Don't forget to send a thank you note to the reporter when your story runs. The key is to develop a long-term, trusting relationship with the media.

Here are three steps to help you leverage the local press coverage your school receives:

1. **Capture and archive the media.** Having a story about your school run on TV or in the newspaper is only the first step. Here's how to convert a news spot to a video on your **school website** to ensure that your school community will be able to watch the coverage at their convenience.

   - *From offline.* First, use iRecord, a personal media recorder that records video and audio on a USB drive from your TV, to record the local newscast. If you are not able to access a copy of the recorded broadcast, you can also order a DVD version of the story from the station. Using the free computer application Handbrake, you can convert the DVD into a YouTube-friendly file on your computer's hard drive.

   - *To online.* Next, plug the USB stick into a computer and upload the video to your **YouTube** account. This will allow your subscribers to watch the video and searchers to find the coverage online.

   - *To your website.* Once the video footage from the local newscast is on YouTube, use the "embed codes" to post the media on your school website.

2. **Share links to the media.** If the newspaper or TV news media posts stories about your school online, be sure to include links to this original content on your website and all of your **social media** pages. Also, **comment** on the stories and include a link back to your school. If possible, include a link to **student blogs** or your story on the school website. All of these back-and-forth links will help increase your **school's online presence** and search engine results.

3. **Post your own versions online.** In an age of media sharing, most news outlets are allowing their video content to be embedded on other websites. If your local press hasn't caught up with this sharing trend, or if they have removed the video of your story, ask for permission to use it on your own website or to post it on **Flickr** or YouTube.

Reflecting on the Day

To complete our service learning day, I asked all of the students to **e-mail** me their reflections on the day. Many students also posted their reflections online on their **student portfolio** or on the blog section of their **Ning** profile. Having students post their reflections is a great way to continue the conversation about the event with both members of your school and your students' extended network.

You might also post your experiences and reflections on your own **YouTube channel** or **school leader's blog.** This is also a great place to thank the nonprofits and media outlets.

Of all the tools in our **social media** toolbox, **Facebook** seemed to have the most impact and generate the most community interaction. We used Facebook to post the announcement about the event; post pictures and updates during the event; and post links to online media, including news coverage after the event. As a school leader beginning to use social media, focus on improving your Facebook presence. This one tool alone can have a dramatic impact on your school.

RECRUITING, SCREENING, AND HIRING TEACHERS

As has been discussed in previous chapters, social media can also be a great way to find innovative, tech-savvy teachers to bring into your school. This case study demonstrates how to use all of your social media tools together to achieve this goal.

The Tools We Use

Hiring great teachers today requires using **social media** in many ways. To recruit, screen, and hire our incredible teaching staff, we use many of the tools outlined in this book to engage candidates in the hiring process. We used our **school website,** an **online survey form, craigslist, LinkedIn, YouTube,** and **multiposting services** in the hiring process:

- **School website.** Hiring teachers using social media starts with your school website. Remember that your school website is your anchor on the Internet. It is the main place to which all search engine traffic will be led. When advertising available positions, ensure that you have all of the information on your website. You may want to include the job description, an explanation of how to apply, and any other additional information candidates will need. In our own hiring process we even created an introductory video directed to teacher candidates, which we embedded on our jobs page on our website.

- **Online survey form.** You can embed an online survey form on your website. Having interested candidates fill out this form, as opposed to asking them simply to e-mail a résumé, will help you and your human resources department better manage the incoming applicants. An online survey form with applicants' contact information, years of experience, certification status, and any other information that might help you filter candidates will give you easy access to information to better determine which of them to offer an interview. You might even include short answer or essay boxes to help screen out less serious candidates. Ask applicants to describe their own teaching philosophy or to give an overview of their classroom management strategy. The more you can get to know your candidates before scheduling interviews, the less time you'll waste in the end. You'll also have more informed questions if they do make it to the interview stage. The information from your form is also downloadable into an Excel spreadsheet. You can sort candidates based on the subject area they teach, their certification status, their years of experience, and so on. This database will be especially helpful when you need to fill positions in the future.

- **Craigslist.** This site has overshadowed local newspaper classified ads as the number one place to advertise local teaching positions. Best of all, craigslist is free. It allows HTML, which means that your online ad can include clickable links, embedded pictures, and differing font sizes—all of which help your school stand out among the various companies advertising on craigslist. Linking the craigslist ad to your job page on your school website and including your online survey form constitute a great strategy to engage potential candidates.

- **LinkedIn.** This is *the* online platform for professional networking. LinkedIn has many features that help you find the best candidates online, whether you do so by creating a LinkedIn ad to advertise your open positions, using the power of LinkedIn networking to update your school profile page, or making direct contact with potential applicants.

- **YouTube.** People love video. If possible, you will want to be sure to embed an overview video about your school on all of your online job postings. At the time of this writing, craigslist does not allow embedded YouTube videos, but you can place a screenshot image of your YouTube video with a link to that video online. Ads that include an overview video have garnered quite a bit of attention for our school because they help our school's ads stand out from the rest of the crowd on craigslist. This video also helps us better communicate our message and explain the type of candidate we are looking for.

- **Multiposting services.** Finally, ensure that you use the power of your networks to advertise all teaching positions. Include a section in your **eNewsletter** when your hiring season is approaching that links to the job section on your website. Post regular updates on your school's **Facebook** page and **Twitter** accounts. Change your **e-mail** signature to include a link to the jobs page, encouraging recipients to view available jobs at your school.

Screening Candidates with Social Media

When you receive a résumé from an applicant, don't be afraid to use the Internet to find out more information about that person. Information you find online may validate or directly contradict what the candidate has stated in his or her application. Often you'll be able to find links to candidates' **social media** profiles, including their **Facebook** page, **Twitter** profile, and **Google+** account. You can find the answers to numerous questions you might have about candidates through their social media usage, including

- How many friends do they have, and how often do they update their social networks?
- Do they post links to professional articles or resources?
- Are they connected to experts in the field?
- What schools have they attended?
- Are they presenting at any conferences?

Because you can determine a lot by visiting a candidate's **social media** pages, don't be afraid to ask for his or her username or for a link to his or her social networking profiles. Include this question on your **online survey form,** adding a section for a **Facebook** profile, **LinkedIn** address, **Twitter** username, and other links. Make it a regular practice to ask for this information from job applicants.

You might also consider friending job applicants on **Facebook.** This may be the only way you can view their Facebook page, as most savvy **social media** users have their privacy settings enabled. Gaining access to their Facebook will help you better understand who they are, their values, and how they present themselves online.

Making the Call (or Not)

There have been occasions on which I have **googled** the name of an applicant, viewed his **Facebook** page or other information online, and decided not to pursue him further. The person he was projecting online and the way that he represented himself did not seem to be a good fit for the kind of person we were looking for to teach our students. Selecting a teacher is a value judgment, so while being sure to follow all applicable laws, gather as much information as possible about the candidates. You are placing your students, vulnerable children, in the care of each new teacher. The more you know about an applicant, the better decision you can make. It is imperative that you learn as much as possible about him because it is your responsibility to decide whether or not this candidate will influence your students on a daily basis. Some job applicants have issues with this, citing privacy concerns, but with the average Facebook user having 130 friends that can see his or her profile (facebook.com/press/info.php?statistics), one has to wonder if anything they post on Facebook is really private anymore.

GRANT FUNDING WITH SOCIAL MEDIA

Social media tools are a dynamic means of locating, applying for, and tracking grant funding. This section outlines specific methods your school can follow to better use social media tools to assist in growing your school's funding base. You can use social media tools to locate, manage, update, track, announce, and implement grant funding. Acquiring funding is a relational process. You are communicating your school's story and making connections with granters who share your values. Leverage your social media tools to improve your chances of engaging these donors.

Locating Grant Sources

The first step in receiving grant funding is to locate potential opportunities.

1. **Start with a Google search of applicable foundations.** View their grant requirements and sign up for **e-mail** notifications of new funding cycles.

2. **Create a Google alert.** Google Alerts lets you set up specific keywords to notify you through e-mail when a particular keyword pops up on a website or in the news. This allows you to track new notices of funding sources. You can, for example, visit a website of a foundation that traditionally posts information about its upcoming grant schedule and set up an alert to receive information about that site as soon as it has been updated. You can also use Google Alerts to track press releases and news releases, so that you are made aware of funding opportunities as soon as they are available. This places your school in a more competitive position, because you are receiving information in a timely way and are able to respond to grant opportunities with enough notice and time to formulate a compelling grant application.

3. **Use Twitter.** Twitter is primarily a news and link sharing service. Search Twitter for funding opportunities. There are several tools that now allow you to set up an alert for Twitter. Many foundations and granters are postings links to new grants and funding availability through their Twitter account. Setting up a Twitter notification allows you to discover grant sources that you might not have found otherwise.

Managing the Grant Writing Process

Writing grants can now become a more social experience. Your school can benefit from the collaborative tools now available for free to school leaders and classroom teachers. Use **social media** tools to support classroom teachers in the grant writing process. **E-mail** a link to an **online survey form** to request specific information from your teachers for DonorsChoose.org, the Target foundation, the Best Buy Foundation, and other organizations. Many of these foundations have small classroom implementation grants of a few thousand dollars. By creating a form for your teachers to fill out with a specific deadline and notification settings, you can encourage your classroom teachers to apply for these grants. Further, you can use **Google Docs** to allow a committee to edit the application instead of solely relying on one person to write and submit it. By subdividing the work across a number of faculty members and establishing tracking protocols and responsibilities, you can benefit from more efficiently managing the grant writing process and repurposing grant content for future applications. The more you use collaborative tools in the writing process, the more likely you are to receive funding, as more teachers will be encouraged to apply for grants because of the lessened workload afforded by such tools.

Updating Your School Website

One of the key elements to receiving grant funding is positioning your school through your **school website** and **social media** presence in a way that helps make your school fundable. Even the smallest schools and nonprofits can afford to create a professional website. After you have spoken with potential granters, your website is the first place they check to establish the credibility of the school. Many granters will never even visit your school, so your website is their primary way of gathering information about your school. If your website is outdated or unattractive, you may be missing out on opportunities for funding. Remember, there are always more people requesting funding than the amount of funding available. Therefore, grant committees are constantly looking for a reason to turn down an applicant school. Your website should not be the reason you are being rejected for grant funding.

Use grant questions to help write the content for your **school website.** Many grant questions are common across foundation applications. Questions about the mission and vision of your school, about your school's goals, and about the students that your school serves are fairly standard, so be sure to include them on your website. The granter will use your website to verify the information you have stated in the grant application. Include key information granters look for on the "about" page of your website, and your school will be better positioned as a candidate to receive grant funding.

Tracking Grant Application Deadlines

Using collaborative tools to track grant applications can be an effective means of using **social media.** The challenge for school leaders is that it is easy for them to get caught up in the day-to-day operations of the school, neglecting the big picture—including the need to fund programs for their school's future success. Establishing a clear tracking system through **Google Calendar** will help ensure that more grants are applied for. Create a grant application calendar, setting three dates:

1. The date of the initial grant committee meeting
2. The deadline for the final application review by an administrator
3. The deadline for submitting the grant

Establishing these dates on a calendar will help ensure that they are not neglected. Often successfully receiving grant funding is simply a numbers game. Applying for three grants puts you in a different position than applying for one hundred grants. If you receive even 10 percent of the grants you apply for, applying for one hundred puts you in a much better position than simply applying for three grants. In your grant application shared calendar, you might also include dates for following up a few days, two weeks, and a month after submitting the application. Being notified of when to follow up will help place your school in a better position to receive funding.

Announcing Grant Awards

Once your school receives grant funding, use the tips and tricks you have learned in this book to share the good news with your community. The leverage provided by receiving grant funding will help your school stand out from the competition, allowing you to capitalize on other grant opportunities and community goodwill. Often, when a school receives grant funding, it has no strategic way to share that information with the community. Now you can share this news on your **school website,** on your **Facebook** profile, on **Twitter,** and in your **eNewsletter.** You can even make a **YouTube** video to show how your school will be using the funding to help students. It is up to you, as the school leader, to share your story of grant funding. Here are a few specific ways that we have used:

- **Public relations efforts.** Write a press release announcing the grant funding. This will help you get local media coverage, get the name of your school out into the community, and look good for the foundation giving the grant.
- **School website.** Ensure that you announce the grant funding in a primary location on your website. You want everyone in your community to know

about your grant funding. This will generate excitement and encourage members of your school community to further invest in your school.

- **Twitter and Facebook.** These tools provide interactive opportunities to share the news of your school funding. Look for ways to link back to the foundation and its giving site. Thank them frequently through Twitter. "Thank you to @ foundation_name for your generous support of @mentorshipbr" is a nice way to announce the support on Twitter and also to directly thank the granter. Most foundations now have a key staff member managing their **social media** presence. Thanking this foundation through your social media pages will help establish further goodwill and set your school up for a good relationship for future foundation giving. Mentioning foundations through your social media pages before applying for these gifts can also help set your school apart in the application process. When a grant committee knows that they will be receiving an application from your school, they begin to look forward to that application and psychologically set your school apart from the rest of the crowd of schools seeking funding.

Implementing Grant Programs

Consider how you might use **social media** tools to track the implementation of the grant funding. Many foundations offer annual funding and appreciate your tracking how the funds have been used throughout the year. Tracking the implementation of funds efficiently is an appropriate practice that helps put your school in a better position for receiving funds in the future. Use **Google Calendar** to create a shared calendar, or use **online project management software,** such as **Manymoon** (which is integrated with **Google Apps**), to help your school better track the implementation of the grant funds. When you have an efficient structure for reporting to the giving foundation, you continue to build trust, and the granter will see you as a reliable and accountable partner in the venture that it is passionate about. Providing these data in an efficient and effective way can help better position your school to receive funding in subsequent years.

SOLICITING DONATIONS WITH SOCIAL MEDIA

There has never been a better time to advocate for donations to your school. With budget cuts across the nation, it is now important for all school leaders and classroom teachers to pursue private external funding for their school and their classroom. **Social media** tools provide several methods you can employ when seeking to acquire donations for your school. These include direct outreach, affiliate programs, and online donation sites.

Direct Outreach

Use **social media** to build relationships with community leaders and your donor network. Reaching out to and building relationships with granters helps place your school in a more fundable position. Here are a few specific ways to directly reach out to granters. All of these methods help you build relationships with key decision makers. This will allow you to make a direct funding request to the appropriate person when the time comes.

- **Using Twitter.** Follow local luminaries using Twitter. **Comment** on their posts. Ask them direct questions.

- **Using Facebook.** Friend community leaders on Facebook. Share key information with them, and invite them to events that you are hosting at your school.

- **Using Skype.** Use a videoconferencing platform such as Skype to host guest speakers in your classrooms. Often getting a potential donor to volunteer is the first step in engaging him or her.

- **Communicating face-to-face.** Never forget the value of a personal connection. Be sure to attend local events to build relationships with community leaders. Once you've met them in person, ask for their permission to add them to your **eNewsletter.** Send a "community news" version of your eNewsletter about once a month to continue engaging these leaders. Also be sure to attend any events that they are hosting and, if possible, volunteer to assist at these events. Show that you care about what they are doing in your local community. One local donor at our school is a large supporter of the United Way. We are sure to volunteer for this organization's annual gala, offering to sell tickets, greet guests, and serve the tables. These efforts alone have had a big impact on this donor because we show that we care about the same issues. When she is considering the next nonprofit to donate to, we want our school to be the first organization she thinks about. These events not only encourage a spirit of volunteerism in our students and introduce them to other community leaders but also help our school stay top of mind when this granter is looking for a nonprofit to give to.

- **Commenting.** For community leaders who have **blogs** (and many now do), be sure to regularly visit and post comments. Even the most popular bloggers personally read comments left on their site.

Affiliate Programs

The Internet provides many unique opportunities to raise funds for your school. One of these methods is **affiliate programs.** An affiliate program comes into play when someone goes to your **school website** and clicks a link that takes them to another website where they can make a purchase. The owner of the website where the purchase was made gives you, the affiliate, a commission of the eventual sale from your click-through. As an example, **Amazon,** the world's largest online retailer, has an affiliate program that easily integrates with your **social media** platforms. Although numbers fluctuate, their commission percentage is between 4 percent and 6 percent on gross sales. Whenever you mention a book, technology tool, or other product on your social media platforms, include your unique affiliate link to that page in the post. Your school will receive a commission from every purchase made through that link. Amazon even has online tools to allow you to create special banners for your school website featuring books you choose (see Figure 16.1).

Online Donation Sites

Another way for you to make money for your school on the Internet is through **eBay Giving,** the nonprofit arm of eBay. Members of the community that sell merchandise on eBay can designate a percentage of the sale of their auction items to a registered nonprofit. Here are the steps to setting up eBay Giving:

1. **Sign up as a nonprofit.** Simply sign up online and fax a letter on official letterhead to eBay. The approval process takes about two weeks. Once your school is approved, you appear on a searchable list of approved eBay Giving affiliates.

2. **Partner with eBay sellers.** Someone in the community who sells on eBay finds out that he or she can add you as a benefactor to his or her auctions.

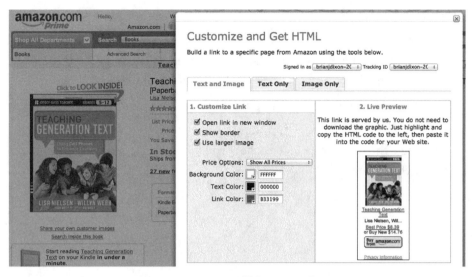

Figure 16.1 Screenshot: Amazon Affiliate Link

Businesses are always looking for tax deductions. Adding your nonprofit can help them simplify their company giving. As they're listing their items, there is actually a check-box for eBay Giving; they simply click on the eBay Giving check-box, search for your school, click on that, and add you as a benefactor to their auction.

3. **Promote partner auctions.** You then can use your school's **social media** links to promote their eBay auctions. This increased exposure may help add to the auction price, ultimately benefiting your school because it receives a percentage of the sale.

As you can see, there are many opportunities to promote your school, hire teachers, and find funding using social media that were not previously possible.

GETTING STARTED WITH SOCIAL MEDIA

Question for Reflection: How might you use the methods discussed in this chapter to improve your grant application process?

First Steps

1. Visit your school website and evaluate it from the perspective of a potential donor. What needs to be updated or changed to encourage you to donate to the school?

2. Create a Google alert for the phrase "accepting grant applications." Apply to grants that fit your school.

3. Google the names of a few teachers you work with to see what parents can see when they search online.

Internet Safety

Given the concern many school leaders have over student safety online, this book would be incomplete without a chapter on Internet safety, particularly in regard to students accessing technology at school. This chapter outlines the dangers students face online and offers strategies to keep students protected.

DANGERS ONLINE

The world has changed. The dangers that students are now facing are much different from those they confronted just a few years ago due to the advances in technology. Almost all students now have the Internet in their pocket. This allows them to access explicit content, participate in cyberbullying, have inappropriate relationships, and use mobile devices to engage in explicit text messaging known as "sexting":

- **Accessing and sharing explicit content online.** This can include viewing and sharing content that is legally restricted for those under the age of eighteen.

- **Cyberbullying.** A recent phenomenon with the accessibility of the Internet and the ability to post multimedia online is a new level of bullying called cyberbullying. Now that students are easy to find through YouTube, Facebook, student blogs, instant messaging, and other tools, most students can no longer hide their real identity online. The pictures and the videos they post are identifiable as theirs. All of this transparency can lead to authentic conversations, but it can also cause great harm for students because people online do not perceive the need to have accountability. Students who are particularly vulnerable include social outcasts and those who are mentally challenged, but any student can be a victim of cyberbullying. When students make fun of each other in a relentless, degrading fashion online, this content is publicly posted, and it can seem like the end of the world to a teenager. Some suicides across the country have reportedly been linked to cyberbullying.

- **Engaging in inappropriate relationships.** This includes relationships with online predators, inappropriate relationships between students and teachers, and online relationships with unknown peers. Having an Internet friend is quickly becoming a normal kind of relationship, but, just as in real life, such a relationship can become detrimental. Parents and educators should discuss with students the possible problems that can arise from online interaction.

- **Sexting.** This is posting or sharing content that is of an adult nature. Sexting can also involve students' taking pictures of themselves in explicit positions and sending their picture to their classmates. Often these pictures end up online, as several websites are now dedicated to hosting these explicit pictures of teens. Sexting is probably the most dangerous behavior in which students can participate using a mobile device. As technology continues to grow, some students may not ever be able to escape from the fact that they took that type of picture and put it online. Conducting Internet safety training that explains the seriousness of sexting to students is an important role for school staff. If you have not already, meet with your guidance department to consider ways to teach your students about the dangers and long-term consequences of sexting.

SIX SAFETY STEPS

Helping students stay safe online requires a community approach. Use the follow strategies:

Start Small

As with any new venture, begin one step at a time, learn the lessons, and experience successes growing from there. Start with one technology tool, perhaps student portfolios. It can be tempting to dive right into the deep end of social media, but this would be foolish. Starting small with one technology tool enables you to get the training and support you need before using that tool with students. Ask any questions you have so that you feel confident before integrating new technology into your school.

Get Trained

When adopting a new technology tool, ensure that students and teachers have adequate training. Knowing a tool well will help ensure that the focus stays on learning. Participating in ongoing professional development is now easier than ever. With frequent teleseminars and webinars delivered on demand; with archived training tools online, such as Slideshare presentations and YouTube tutorials; and with the countless online articles and e-books that are downloadable with only a few clicks, learning about and implementing social media across your schoolwide practice is now easier than ever. Here are a few of the best ways to learn and teach others about social media:

Build a Partner Network

One effective strategy in managing social media, particularly when it comes to students and their safety, is to build a network of community-based partners that can help assist you in times of difficulty, such as

- **The sheriff's department.** The police have an Internet task force specially trained in handling issues involving cyberbullying, online predators, and sexting. Reaching out to this task force is an essential step in building a partner network to best serve your students.

- **Internet safety nonprofits.** There are many local, regional, and national nonprofits established to help keep children safe on the Internet. Some offer their services for free, as they have received grant funding, and others charge for their workshops. Contracting their help may just be worth it to protect your students. Some examples of Internet safety nonprofits include

- *i-SAFE,* a nonprofit organization that focuses on teaching students to be safe, responsible, and productive in their use of the Internet
- *Childnet International,* a nonprofit organization that produces videos teaching students how to stay safe online
- *Web Wise Kids,* a national nonprofit organization that helps promote a culture of safety, respect, and responsibility by providing resources to equip students to navigate the Internet safely

Reach out to these groups to see what services they might be able to provide to your school: consultation, faculty training, or a student workshop.

Become an Expert

Understanding such tools as Facebook and Twitter and becoming knowledgeable about online safety are important for your role as a school leader. Learning more about this topic isn't complicated. Reading this book has been a worthy start. In fact, it has been said that if you read the three most popular books in a specific field, you can be considered an expert in that field. You'll probably know more about that topic than 99 percent of the population. Consider what gaps still exist in your knowledge and search out other books that you could read to help you become an Internet and social media expert. Often googling your question will lead you to great online resources to help you.

Pursue Training Resources

In addition to this book, here are three great resources to access:

- **YouTube.** The quality of tutorials on YouTube is surprisingly high. All of these are free and searchable. If, for example, you'd like to learn about privacy settings on Facebook, go to YouTube, type in "privacy settings Facebook," and choose from among several videos to watch. Using screenshots, these videos outline specific step-by-step instructions for adjusting your privacy settings on Facebook.

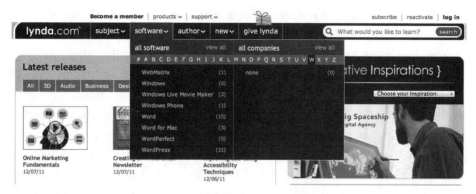

Figure 17.1 Screenshot: Lynda.com

- **Lynda.com.** This online subscription service offers professional video training on various technology topics. Although lynda.com is most used for learning new software programs, it also has great videos on brand management and identity, safety online, and other emerging topics in the technology space (see Figure 17.1).

- **AppSumo.** For the advanced technology users who already have a grasp of key technological concepts, I highly recommend AppSumo. The founder of AppSumo, Noah Kagan, regularly interviews high-level experts in the fields of Internet branding, marketing, productivity, and design. Packages include downloadable video and audio versions of these conversations, transcripts, and PowerPoint slides. You have to pay for individual courses, many ranging from twenty-five to seventy-five dollars, but for very niche content that could have a dramatic impact on your leadership practice, the dollar amount can be worth it.

Hire Great Faculty and Staff

Hire a competent and student-centered director of technology. It is important that your technology staff have both expertise in the field and a love of working with students. The purpose of monitoring technology use at school is not to catch students breaking rules, but to educate them to use technology wisely in a safe environment. Because there is no 100 percent foolproof system, student-centered staff members are needed to take the time to train teachers, talk to students, and collaborate with parents when things go awry.

Your faculty and staff can make all the difference in handling difficult issues at your school. How your school deals with Internet safety and student use of computing technology—including mobile devices—can be dramatically affected by the quality and perspective of your team. In the hiring process, consider asking questions about the prospective teacher's view of technology. Many teachers that are new to the profession use technology in their daily life, yet they struggle to find ways to use technology in the classroom. Finding teachers who understand the value of student-centered learning, whereby students are using real-world technology in authentic ways, is probably the best strategy you can implement to be sure that your students effectively use technology in a safe way.

When you, as a school leader, roll out a new initiative, a key to the success of that initiative is always teacher buy-in. Teachers need to believe in the purpose and plan of that strategic objective, or else it will fail even before it has begun. Screening teachers for their perspective on technology use can help you better implement changes to technology use plans and policies as the technology continues to develop.

Teach Parents

Your parents need to be partners. You want to partner with parents to be on the same page, and to better understand how today's technology affects students: their safety, their social development, their peer relationships, their homework, their future work life, and their current schooling. Here are three ways you can help parents understand Internet safety issues:

- **Host seminars.** Empower your parents by hosting an Internet safety seminar. An effective speaker will teach parents about the dangers online and answer questions they have.

- **Share articles in your eNewsletters.** In each of your weekly eNewsletters, include a brief excerpt and a link to a relevant Internet safety article. Some great resources to check out are NetSmartz and the blog *SafetyClicks*.

- **Answer questions.** In the parent group on your online collaborative network (Ning) or on a parent feedback section of your school website, give parents the opportunity to ask questions about their child's online safety.

Use Group Policing

Effectively using social media across your school will require a group policing approach, with many members of your school helping to manage the appropriateness of the content being shared online. As an example, the online collaborative network Ning allows for a flagging option, empowering your users (students and faculty) to note inappropriate content. Formalizing this process can help you better manage the detrimental content that is bound to find its way onto your online collaborative network; and implementing a group policing system is the most effective way to ensure the balance of fostering a collaborative community of student creation while also maintaining accountability for the content. This strategy has been used by the large technology players, including Facebook and YouTube, and it can also work for your school. The following strategies can help you implement group policing:

- **Empower your faculty.** Give your teachers administrative rights to approve and delete content. This will help ensure that you are not the only one viewing content for appropriateness on your online collaborative network.

- **Form a student technology team.** With a select group of students who are passionate about using next-generation technology across their school, you can take advantage of the power of crowdsourcing, whereby multiple people are helping to regulate the content. The last thing you want to do is stay up until 2:00 a.m. deleting inappropriate photos from your school network. Find student helpers to assist you in managing the schoolwide collaborative network.

- **Use an Acceptable Use Policy (AUP).** A must in today's school environment is a clear AUP. Timely follow-up with consequences for violations of the AUP is crucial. Clearly outlining what is acceptable and what is not is the important first step in using any technology at your school. Most school districts already have an AUP in place, so the next step would be to review it for appropriateness and to modify what needs to be changed. Often these documents are written at the district level, approved by attorneys, and mandated from the superintendent without much input from school administrators, let alone classroom teachers, students, or parents.

AUPs have shifted from the basic printing policies and rules of accessing the Internet to philosophical statements about student creation, fair use, copyright, and sharing. Essentially, these are statements concerning educational values that have been created by noneducators. In training seminars and workshops I conduct, I have school administrators design their own AUP, outlining what they consider to be acceptable use and inappropriate use. After a brainstorming session designing an AUP, we then review the actual AUP from each administrator's district and are often surprised to find how diametrically opposed the underlying philosophies of these documents can be.

Build a Culture of Collaboration

Students need to feel that they can report what is happening online, particularly when a situation has gotten out of control. With students' feeling such a personal connection to their computer, it can seem like a violation to report a problem to school administrators. Find ways to build a culture of trust. Moving through the AUP creation process, administrators I regularly work with discover that their school policies are not encouraging a schoolwide culture of collaboration. They realize that the social media tools that are now available for free on any device help create the possibility of the educational utopia that led them into the classroom in the first place. Students are engaging with real-world resources and are creating original content in projects to inspire others to effect lasting change. This is the opportunity to move from static read-the-text and take-the-quiz education to an active process of discovering text, bringing the text to life, empowering students, creating original work, advocating for a social cause, and presenting to an authentic community. These social media tools now make such educational activities not only possible but also practical. Creating a collaborative community is possible if you do the following:

- **Embrace project-based learning (PBL).** PBL fundamentally shifts the balance of power in the classroom from teacher-delivered instruction to student-centered project creation. When done well, PBL is an authentic way for students to master classroom concepts while building their "soft skills," including critical thinking, problem solving, teamwork, and advocacy. Some great resources for implementing PBL are the George Lucas Foundation, whose Edutopia website makes available a wealth of videos highlighting the best practices of educators across the nation, and the Buck Institute of Education.

- **Celebrate student work.** Post student work publicly. Invite community members into the school to serve on project panels. When possible, post student work outside of the school community. Display student work at the airport, in law offices, and in medical offices. There are many opportunities to get student work out into the community at large. The more you encourage authentic student work—from film festivals to art exhibits—the more authentic that work will be. This inspires collaboration that goes beyond the classroom, the teacher, and the student, leading into conversations with experts from the field, the parent community, and the community around the school.

- **Provide frequent teacher training.** Classroom teachers are the linchpin in building a culture of collaboration. Teachers are used to teaching with siloed subjects—the history teacher only teaches history, and the math teacher only teaches math. But there is math in history, and there is history in math! By having frequent professional development, collaborative cross-subject planning meetings, and interdisciplinary units, you can encourage your teachers to have larger conversations about building a collaborative community. These collaborations lend themselves to better use of social media. Teachers can easily share their knowledge with other teachers and with students in other classes using Google Docs, websites, e-mail, and Web conferences.

GETTING STARTED WITH INTERNET SAFETY

Questions for Reflection: How safe are your students online? Do they know how to avoid malicious behavior and obscene content?

First Steps

1. Schedule a parent Internet safety training night.

2. Begin sharing Internet safety tips as part of your daily announcements or in your weekly eNewsletters.

Acknowledgments

This book wouldn't be possible without the vision and investment from the dedicated educators I've worked with throughout the years, including Douglas Fisher, Bruce Fast, Deidre Plett, Barbara Freiberg, Henry Fast, Milt Uecker, Allison Rossett, Stacey Simmons, Bernie Dodge, Alexandra Chung Rouse, Larry Rosenstock, Cheryl Mason, Jerry Ammer, Clark Gilbert, Jan Menconi, Jim Hopson, Andre Harris, Jason Askegreen, Dan Ryska, Rob Riordan, Ben Daley, Dan Kohn, Tom Vander Ark, Victoria Bergsagel, the entire Helix Board, and the faculty at Mentorship Academy.

This book is also dedicated to the peers and mentors who have challenged me to grow and take risks, including Ryan Forsthoff, Jared Loftus, Henry Hays, Sean Cangelosi, David Ogwyn, Bob Mackenzie, Hans Googer, Kevin McKee, Mark Foreman, Pasquale Russo, and Lee Rizio.

. . . to the family that has encouraged me along the way, including Larry and Linda Dixon, George and Annette Murray, Amy, Thom, Heather, Dave, Laura, Phil, Casey, Frank, and, of course, Nanny.

. . . to the gurus and authors who made an indelible mark on the content and approach of this book, including Tim Ferriss, Gary Vaynerchuk, Brendon Burchard, Michael Port, Fred Jones, Dave Ramsey, Dan Miller, David Allen, Seth Godin, Ron Clark, Chet Holmes, and Brian Tracy.

. . . to the writing and publishing team that has helped this book become a reality, including Alicia Mundt, Athena Perrakis, Dominique Chatterjee, Matt Holt at Wiley, Kate Bradford at Jossey-Bass, Nana Twumasi, Carol Hartland, Francie Jones, Hunter Stark, and my agent, Bruce R. Barbour.

. . . and to you, the reader, for the many ways you will adopt and adapt these strategies to have an impact on the students you teach and the community you serve.

About the Author

Dr. Brian J. Dixon was raised in the fields of Southern Manitoba, Canada. Dreaming of rock and roll stardom, he believed teaching would be an "easy job with the summers off" to tour the world. His first day in the classroom of a high-needs urban school in South Carolina, however, rocked his world and changed his career path forever. It was that day when he began to discover the power of technology to engage students of all abilities and backgrounds. Over the years that followed Brian has taught at public, private, and charter schools. He was the director of High Tech High Flex, and has a doctoral degree in educational technology from the University of San Diego and San Diego State University. He is the founding principal and executive director of Helix Schools, which runs the Mentorship Academy of Digital Arts and the Mentorship Academy of Science and Technology. He lives in Baton Rouge, Louisiana, with his wife, Julie, a former elementary school teacher, and their son, Ryland. Brian often writes and speaks on technology and future trends in education. He coaches school districts, universities, and nonprofits to help them thoughtfully use social media in their daily practice. To connect with Brian, visit brianjdixon.com or text his cell phone at 225-505-5013.

Index

Page references followed by *fig* indicate an illustrated figure.

engagement through increased, 13, 14*fig*; Facebook for increasing, 26–27*fig*; Google+ for increasing, 208*fig*; LinkedIn for increasing, 191*fig*–192; mobile devices for increasing, 182–183*fig*; Ning for increasing, 73*fig*–74; online surveys for increasing, 101*fig*; school website for increasing, 59–60*fig*; student portfolio for increasing, 142–143*fig*; Twitter for increasing, 46*fig*; YouTube for increasing, 85*fig*, 86. *See also* Dixon Ongoing Social Engagement Model

AwayFind app, 173–174

B

Baeder, Justin, 172
Barrett, Helen, 141
Bing searches, 141
Bingham, Tony, 68
Bit.ly, 219
Blog benefits: casting a leadership vision, 147; growing your platform and career, 149; improving your professional practice, 148–149; influencing the educational community, 148; sharing your school's story, 147
Blog social engagement: advocacy increased through ongoing, 161*fig*, 162; awareness increased through ongoing, 161*fig*; collaboration increased through ongoing, 161*fig*, 162; feedback increased through ongoing, 161*fig*, 162
Blog topic sources: additional ideas for, 153–154; frequently asked questions, 150; idea websites, 153; the local news, 150–151; the national news, 151; other blogs, 151; quotes, 152; searching Twitter to find trending topics, 153; suggestions for finding, 149
Blog writing times: challenge of finding enough, 154–155; establish a daily routine for, 155; first thing in the morning, 155–156; Freedom (macfreedom.com) productivity application for, 156; reflecting in the afternoon commute for, 156; write during your morning commute, 155
Blogger (blog platform), 156, 160
Blogging best practices: keep it appropriate, 159; keep it updated, 159; make it accessible, 160; make it look professional, 159; make it searchable, 160; make it shareable, 161
Blogging platforms: Blogger, 156, 160; building your, 157–158; Drupal, 142; hosting, themes, and plug-ins features of, 156–157; Tumblr, 156, 160. *See also* WordPress
Blogs: benefits of using, 147–149; best practices for, 159–161; common school tasks before and after starting a, 162–163; description of, 2, 146–147; embedding YouTube video clips into your, 158; finding time to write, 154–156; finding topics to write about, 149–154; getting started with your, 164; guidelines for writing, 154; making comments to, 152; microblogs, 2; Ning, 70; ongoing social engagement with school leader's,

161*fig*–162; posting on LinkedIn, 190; screenshot: school leader's blog, 148*fig*; soliciting donations using, 236
Bloomington High School wrestling team (California), 29
Book talks, 210
Broken links, 65
Buck Institute of Education, 246

C

Calendar and appointment management: Calendar app, 171–172; Google calendar for, 127, 132, 225; Google+ for, 210; social media available for event, 225
Calendar apps: agenda attachments, 172; appointment notes, 172; availability sharing, 172; calendar syncing, 171; day planning, 171; meeting invitations, 171; reminder function, 171
Call-Em-All, 180
Catch-all e-mail account, 220
Caven, Debra, 126
Celebrating students: building collaboration by, 247; Facebook used for, 24
Cell phones: parents and school leaders', 177–180; students and, 180–182
Checkbox Online, 96, 97
Childnet International, 242
Children's Internet Protection Act (CIPA), 78
Circles (Google+), 206–207, 209
Classroom 2.0 social network, 5
Classroom portal benefits: authentic assessment, 126; enabling collaboration of teachers and students, 126; enhanced access to students, 125; fewer photocopies, 128; increased engagement, 127; real-world relevance, 127
Classroom portal social engagement: advocacy increased through ongoing, 128*fig*, 129; awareness increased through ongoing, 128*fig*; collaboration increased through ongoing, 128*fig*, 129; feedback increased through ongoing, 128*fig*, 129
Classroom portal tips: evaluate implementation of, 133–134; use Google Apps, 132; offer training resources, 132; sharing best practices with other teachers, 133
Classroom portals: benefits of, 125–128; common school tasks before and after, 129–132; description of, 123–124; features of, 124–125; getting started with, 134; ongoing social engagement with, 128*fig*–129; screenshot: classroom portal, 124*fig*; tips for implementing, 132–134
Classroom portals features: classroom information, 124–125; collaboration tools and multimedia sharing, 125; downloadable documents, 125; user management, 125
Classrooms: flipped, 90; using online surveys in the, 105; using YouTube in the, 88–91
Collaboration: blog for increasing, 161*fig*, 162; celebrating student work to build, 247; classroom

E-mail screenshots: Inbox, 110*fig*; No New Mail, 112*fig*; Review Stars, 112*fig*; Select All, 110*fig*; Star Important, 111*fig*

E-mail signatures, 18

E-mail social engagement: advocacy increased through ongoing, 119*fig*, 121; awareness increased through ongoing, 119*fig*–120; collaboration increased through ongoing, 119*fig*, 120–121; feedback increased through ongoing, 119*fig*, 120

E-mails: asking for information from grant sources, 231; asking students to send reflections on events via, 227; AwayFind app for, 173–174; catch-all e-mail account for, 220; Google Alerts set up to alert you via, 231; mobile devices for sending, 173; school rules regarding, 116–119; schoolwide community service day information sent by, 224; spam, 17, 114

"Eat that frog" productivity concept, 155–156

Eat That Frog (Tracy), 155

eBay actions, 236–237

eBay Giving, 236

Education Week, 72, 151, 196

Edudemic, 194, 207

Edutopia, 16, 29, 129, 133, 246

Emergency alert system: broadcasting message across networks, 180; using e-mail for parents, 120; mobile devices used as part of, 179–180; sending text blast, 180; TextMarks tool for, 179–180. *See also* Messages

eNewsletter advantages: customizable tools and services as, 12; digital content as, 11–12; intelligent data as, 12–13

eNewsletter content: advantages of digital, 11–12; archiving, 11; call readers to action with, 17; using compelling e-mail subject line, 16; don't bury the headline, 16; offer value through, 17; using pictures, 16

eNewsletter social engagement: advocacy component of, 14*fig*, 15; collaboration component of, 14*fig*; feedback component of, 14*fig*; increased awareness component of, 13, 14*fig*

eNewsletter tasks: archiving content, 11; collecting your contact list, 10; communicating information to specific groups, 15; comparing traditional newsletter tasks and, 15; resending the eNewsletter as needed, 11; sending the eNewsletter, 10, 15; tracking recipients' interactions, 10, 13, 15; writing the eNewsletter, 10

eNewsletters: advantages of, 11–13; best practices for, 16–18; comparing traditional newsletter and, 15; description of, 2, 9; Facebook and Twitter links on, 15; getting started with, 18; grant award announcements through, 233; Internet safety articles on, 244; ongoing social engagement through use of, 13–15; reducing your e-mail by unsubscribing from, 114; school tasks before and

after sending, 15; school website providing sign-up form for, 63; soliciting donations using, 235; tasks involved in, 10–11; as tool for hiring great teachers, 229

eNewsletters best practices: avoiding spam, 17; capturing e-mail addresses, 17–18; writing relevant content, 16–17

Epps, Kathy, 73

Events: announcing, 225; blogs used to promote, 150; e-mailed announcements on, 121; Facebook Events to share information on, 24, 25, 31; using Facebook to announce, 31; fishbowl business card contests, 18; LinkedIn to announce, 192, 198; mobile devices used to announce, 171, 175; Ning for announcing, 72, 74; robotics team tournament, 30–31; scheduling, 225; schoolwide community service day case study on promoting, 224–227; sharing, 225; using social media to engage families in, 3; social media tools for planning, 224–225; Twitter used to announce, 42, 44, 48; YouTube used to share, 86, 88

Evernote app, 175–176

F

Facebook: adding your friends on, 21; advanced tech-savvy features of, 37–38; advantages of Ning for collaboration over, 72; asking students to post reflections on event on their account, 227; benefits to school community, 25–26; building leadership credibility through use of, 4; communicating with your friends on, 21; comparing school tasks before and after innovation of, 29–31; connection options on, 21–25; creating your profile on, 20–21; description of, 20; eNewsletters links to, 15; getting started with, 38; grant award announcements through, 233, 234; linking LinkedIn to, 192; Livescribe pen for posting notes to, 184; ongoing social engagement using, 26–29; privacy and safety concerns on, 34–37, 242; school advertising in, 32–34; school's Acceptable Use Policy for students on, 35; soliciting donations using, 235; as tool for hiring great teachers, 229; Twitter compared to, 40

Facebook ad statistics: amount spent on one day of advertising, 34; average cost per click (CPC), 34; click-through rate (CTR), 34; clicks, 33; impressions, 33; social percentage, 33

Facebook ads: creating a, 32–33; measuring return on investment of, 33–34; targeting your, 33

Facebook advanced features: Facebook Places to "check-in," 37–38; iFrames, 37

Facebook app, 174–175

Facebook benefits: accessibility, 25–26; easy to use, 25; manageability, 26; ubiquitous nature, 26

Facebook connections: Facebook Events, 25; Facebook groups, 24; Facebook pages, 22–24

of, 98, 101*fig*–102, 103, 104–105; getting started with, 105; ongoing social engagement with, 100–103; planning , 100; ten steps for successful, 97–99. *See also* Parent survey tasks

P

Painter, Steven, 57
Pappalardo, Gaetan, 42
Parent conferences: classroom portals for scheduling, 132; Google+ for arranging, 210
Parent survey tasks, 103. *See also* Online surveys
"Parent university" night, 35
Parents: using contests to capture e-mail addresses of, 18; using e-mail as part of emergency alert system for, 120; e-mail for teacher communication with, 122; Facebook as facilitating collaboration between students and, 28; Facebook training for, 35; how online surveys are used with, 96; Ning for soliciting feedback from, 76; Ning groups for online collaboration with, 77; providing faculty information to, 63; school leader cell phones and, 177–180; teaching Internet safety to, 244; voicemail hotline provided to, 178–179
Partnership for 21st Century Skills, 69
Passwords: management tips for your, 220; protecting your, 79–80
Personal health apps, 176–177
Photos (Google+), 207
Ping.fm: increasing online presence using, 218–219; linking LinkedIn using, 192; for multimedia sharing, 158
Plagiarism, 141
Poestenkill Elementary School (New York), 44
Press coverage: converting news post to video on your school website, 226; grant award announcements through press release and, 233; leveraging for your school service day, 226–227; post your own versions of news coverage online, 227; sharing news stories on your school events to local news, 226; uploading news post to your YouTube account, 226
Principals. *See* School leaders
Principals and Teachers Network, 198
Privacy issues: Facebook, 34–35; YouTube tutorial on Facebook, 242
Productivity: "eat that frog" concept of, 155–156; Freedom (macfreedom.com) tool for increased, 156; mobiles devices used to increase your, 168–177
Professional development: how a blog helps with your, 149; LinkedIn used for, 196–199; mobile devices used to facilitate, 176; Twitter 140-character tool used for, 49
Profiles: asking students to post reflections on event on their own, 227; Facebook, 20–21, 36, 229–230; Google+ (or Google Plus), 204–205; LinkedIn, 190–191; Ning, 70; screenshot of, 189*fig*; student

portfolio "about me" page, 136*fig*; Twitter, 229; for your school on LinkedIn, 200
Project-based learning (PBL), 246
Promoting service day. *See* Schoolwide community service day case study
Provenzano, Nicholas, 127

Q

Quotes: as blog topic source, 152; screenshot: Amazon Highlights as source for finding, 152*fig*

R

Rate, Nick, 45
Recruiting teachers. *See* Teacher hiring process
Registration e-mail forms, 17
Retweets (RT), 43
Ring, Sara, 133
Robotics team tournaments: announcing event before and after Facebook, 31; fundraising before and after Facebook, 31; hosting year-end banquet before and after Facebook, 31; promoting tasks before and after Facebook, 30
Roner, Shawn, 24

S

SafeShare.TV, 92
Safety. *See* Internet safety
SafetyClicks blog, 244
Salem School District (Oregon), 27
Salsbury, Marina, 207
Scheduling. *See* Calendar and appointment management
School administrators. *See* School leaders
School calendar, 64
School community: benefits of eNewsletters for, 11–13; benefits of Facebook for, 25–26; benefits of social media for, 3–4; how social media builds relationships within, 4; school website for engaging your, 54–55
School culture: Internet safety by building collaborative, 246–247; social media for building collaborative, 3–4. *See also* Social engagement
School leader cell phones: providing your number to parents, 177–178; text messaging with, 178; voicemail hotline, 178–179
School leader commentaries: Ann Hadley on blogs, 151; Carl Anderson on student cell phones, 182; Eric Sheninger on blogs, 147; Eric Sheninger on Facebook, 22; Eric Sheninger on Twitter, 41; Gary Vaynerchuk on blogs, 150; Jeff Dunn on LinkedIn, 194; Justin Baeder on mobile devices, 172; Kimberly Moritz on blogs, 162; Leigh Jones on Twitter as classroom tool, 182; Lisa Nielsen and Willyn Webb on student cell phones, 181; Norman Maynard on blogs, 150; Scott McLeod on blogs, 162; Stephen Jones's use of LinkedIn, 198; Steven Lowder on mobile apps, 183

by, 2–3; description and categories of, 2; getting started with, 237–238. *See also* Dixon Ongoing Social Engagement Model; *specific media tool*

Social media barriers: school or district policy as, 5; student safety issues as, 5; technophobic teachers and school leaders, 5

Social media case studies: grant funding with social media, 230–234; promoting schoolwide community service day, 224–227; recruiting, screening, and hiring teachers, 227–230; soliciting donations with social media, 234–237

Social media links, 63

Social networks: building Internet safety partner network, 241–242; Classroom 2.0, 5; description of, 2; increasing your online presence by signing up for multiple, 217; Ning as collaborative, 68–80; Steve Hargadon on teacher use of, 5. *See also specific media tool*

"Soft ask," 200–201

Spam: avoiding eNewsletters, 17; definition of, 17; marking unwanted messages as, 114

Sparks (Google+), 205, 207

Squeeze page, 65–66

Staff Internet safety expertise, 243–244

Standardized e-mail signatures, 118–119

Student absences, 131

Student cell phones: e-mail on, 181; mobile polls taken using, 182; note-taking apps for, 181; portfolio updates on, 182; school policies on, 180–181; to-do apps for, 181

Student-created video projects, 90

Student Facebook reminders, 23

Student handbook distribution, 62

Student online activity monitoring, 36–37

Student portfolio best practices: address plagiarism, 141; attend to frequency concerns, 140–141; planned rollout, 140

Student portfolios: authentic assessment using, 139–140, 141; benefits of using, 137–140; best practices for using, 140–141; description of, 135–136; features of, 136*fig*–137; getting started with, 144; media literacy skills improved through, 140; mobile devices for updating, 182; ongoing social engagement with, 142–144; technology tips for using, 142

Student portfolios features: "about me" page (student profile), 136*fig*; learning goals list, 137; online résumé, 137; student-created work, 136–137

Student portfolios social engagement: advocacy increased through ongoing, 143*fig*, 144; awareness increased through ongoing, 142–143*fig*; collaboration increased through ongoing, 143*fig*–144; feedback increased through ongoing, 141, 143*fig*

Student presentations, classroom portals facilitating, 131

Student profiles. *See* Profiles

Student recruiting: increasing your online presence for, 214; student portfolios used as tool for, 139; YouTube used for, 92

Student technology team, 245

Student training: on Facebook use, 36; on Internet safety, 76, 241–243*fig*

Students: celebrating, 24, 247; cell phones and, 180–182; Facebook as facilitating collaboration between parents and, 28; how online surveys are used with, 96; improving media literacy skills of, 140; Ning for providing feedback on work to, 76; online dangers to, 239–240; school's Facebook Acceptable Use Policy for, 35; social media for engaging, 3

SurveyMonkey, 96, 97, 104

Surveys. *See* Online surveys

symbol (or hashtag), 42

T

T-shirt sales, 31

Tag cloud: description of, 57; screenshot: tag cloud created with Wordle, 58*fig*

Teacher classroom portal commentaries: Debra Caven, 126; Elizabeth Delmatoff, 129; Julia Hill, 133; Kechia Williams, 125; Nicholas Provenzano, 127; Sara Ring, 133; Scott Akerson, 126

Teacher e-mail commentaries: James Comer, 120; Lyn Newton, 122; Norris Haynes, 120

Teacher eNewsletter commentaries: Kisu Kuroneko, 14; Roberta Furger, 16; Ron Koehler, 11

Teacher Facebook commentaries: Brittany Fishman, 32; Heather Wolpert-Gawron, 29; Kimberly Melton, 27; Peter Kupfer, 23; Shawn Roner, 24; Steve Johnson, 28

Teacher Google+ commentaries: Marina Salsbury, 207; Mark Lewis, 206

Teacher hiring process: screening candidates with social media, 229–230; social media tools used for, 227–229; social media tools used to help make the decision, 230

Teacher Ning commentaries: Bernie Trilling, 69; Charles Fadel, 69; Kathy Epps, 73; Marcia Conner, 68; Michelle Davis, 72; Tony Bingham, 68

Teacher social networking commentary, 5

Teacher student portfolio commentaries: Helen Barrett, 141; Jessie Thaler, 138

Teacher Twitter commentaries: Chris Wejr, 44; Geatan Papalardo, 42; Nick Rate, 45; Peter DeWitt, 44; Steven Anderson, 46

Teacher website commentaries: Chris Wejr, 55; Heather Carver, 61; Heather Mansfield, 55; Kisu Kuroneko on WordPress, 56; Larry and Virginia Decker, 60; Steven Painter on WordPress, 57

Teacher YouTube commentaries: Darren Nelson, 90; Jennifer Hillner, 87; Nancy Grunewald, 89; Naveen Mahesh, 86

Teachers: e-mail communication between parents and, 122; empowering them to approve and delete

with, 88–92; description of, 82; embedding video clips in your blog, 158; getting started with, 93–94; grant award announcements through, 233; having fun online with, 88; how it works, 82–83; interacting with, 84–85; Internet safety tutorials on, 241, 242; Livescribe pen for posting notes to, 184; ongoing social engagement with, 85*fig*–88; recruiting students with, 92; recruiting teachers with, 93*fig*; school website inclusion of embedded, 63; as tool for hiring great teachers, 227, 229; uploading news post on your service day to your, 226. *See also* Videos

YouTube classroom applications: annotated adventures, 91–92; flipped classroom, 90; inspirational videos, 90–91; student-created projects, 90; video lectures, 89

YouTube social engagement: advocacy increased through ongoing, 85*fig*, 87–88; awareness increased through ongoing, 85*fig*, 86; collaboration increased through ongoing, 85*fig*, 87; feedback increased through ongoing, 85*fig*, 86–87

YouTube Teachers Community, 87